THE POISONOUS PIXIE'S SECOND BOOK OF POETRY
– LOCKDOWN EDITION –

A LYRICAL COLLECTION
OF MUSINGS, THOUGHTS,
EXPERIENCES AND PERCEPTIONS
BY
RACHEL RHODES-PUCKETT

The Poisonous Pixie's Second Book of Poetry: Lockdown Edition

Published 2020 by Rachel Rhodes-Puckett
Copyright © 2020 Rachel Rhodes-Puckett

ISBN: 978 1 78645 431 7

Cover Design:
Rachel Rhodes-Puckett & Debbie McGowan

Formatting/Typesetting:
Beaten Track Publishing,
Burscough, Lancashire.
www.beatentrackpublishing.com

This book is dedicated to my parents, Pamela and John Puckett, to my readers and to all those who know me and who have supported my work – thank you.

Special thanks to my good friends, Katherine Fellowes and Line Djuve-Wood, and to Debbie McGowan for reviewing and helping me to iron out the many creases in my draft manuscript – without whose efforts this book would have been peppered with cheesy emojis and grammatical abominations...

Contents

The Poisonous Pixie's Second Book of Poetry
– Lockdown Edition –

A Drop In The Ocean

Used to like watching TV
Now it just makes me bored
Used to love you and me
When it was fun – how I adored

Now my rhythm's all over the place
And so is my aching head
From too much time
Wasted on someone
Who would rather be in bed

Always too tired or broke it seems
To live life to the full
I'm sitting surrounded by shattered dreams
Feeling an ache I wish would dull

A wasted effort
Too much did I give
This depletion is real
Emptied out through combative

Exchanges and retorts
They say romance is dead
Stillborn with you
From beginning to end

So I take my leave
And throw in the towel
Wipe the slate clean
Before I fall foul

Of another broken heart
Like the pieces of my dreams
Scattered all around me
Unpicked at the seams

Salvaging something from the wreck
That's sinking to the bottom of the ocean bed
A smidgin of that stuff named dignity
That will keep me afloat now at last I am free...

A La Prochaine

Job done
It was time to make tracks
She'd paid her dues
And that was that

The cycle of life
Was moving her on
She didn't belong here
Although it was fun

She yearned for more
Than what was on offer
She'd been reduced
To something improper

She needed to extract herself
From the status quo
This wasn't really her
So she had to go

On to the next
Big adventure
She was seeking out
To avert dementia

To the pastures new
She was yearning for
Knock, knock, knocking
On unopened doors

If she persisted
One may unlock
So she made a plan
After taking stock

For it's not healthy to stagnate
In the same old cycle
In order to grow
One must not spiral

Into the same
Mundane routine
But instead take courage
And spread your wings

And then when the moment
Is upon you and right
Soar into the air
And just take flight!

Advent In Avalon

Winter Solstice
The rebirth of the sun
A time for reflection
Where the red water runs

At the foot of the Tor
A holy place
Sacred and serene
Away from the rat race

If they beckon
You must answer the call
To the well
A source of life force

Replenish your energy
Cleanse and purify
Banish your demons
Held by the light

God is love
And love resides there
Drink from the chalice
And your soul repair

Whatever trials or troubles you
Know that it's a test
Find forgiveness there
Find redemption and rest

Fortify yourself
And receive His benevolent grace
Traverse the healing waters
Barefoot, humble, embraced

Emerge from your chrysalis
In preparation for the next cycle
Redeemed and purified
Protected by St Michael

The dawn of a new decade
Is only days away
The anniversary of the birth
Of Christ we shall celebrate

A time to clean the slate
Begin a brand-new chapter
Intention setting to manifest
A future filled with rapture

Know thyself
And cut thy losses
Sever ties
Yet cultivate riches

Nurture positive influences
Follow your inner bliss
Give thanks for all that radiates
Beauty and happiness

Know that you are blessed
Deserving and worthy
Recognise your divinity
Even though you're presently earthly

Follow Bethlehem's star
To illuminate your path
When weakened pray for Him
To support you with His staff

And then rise again
Like a phoenix from the ashes
Of the purging furnace
That illusion shatters and smashes.

Afloat And Ailing In The Arid Attic

Throat is sore
Glands are up
Banging head
Down on my luck

Confined to my bed
But too hot to sleep
Missing the air con
But for work I'm too weak

Swimming in
My own sweat
Stuck to the sheets
Which are wringing wet

Like a water bed
Or rather a paddling pool
My mattress has become la mer
But it's stifling as opposed to cool

Life in the attic
Is an arduous affair
Sub-Siberian in winter
Sweltering in summer sans any air

Oh, bring me an oscillating fan!
To waft me as I ail
In silver or white but definitely not black
Coordination with décor must prevail

I scour Argos
and Amazon online
But the fans are so plentiful
I cannot decide

Which one to order
And can they deliver?
Oh f**k, they've sold out
That'll teach me to dither!

I'll take a cold shower
If I can muster the strength
To stand for long enough
To get myself drenched

Nay, I'm too frail
At least at the minute
Thus my sweat-sodden bed
Retains me in it

If I could just sleep awhile
Replenish my energy
Of this BO-ridden pit
Could I at last be free

But this lurgy with which I'm afflicted
Coupled with the heat
Is keeping me awake incessantly
Sedate me, oh somebody, please!

I shouldn't complain
It's nice to have sun
But being broiled alive
Isn't very much fun

Thus with the lobster
I utterly empathise
So torturous and barbaric
A way to meet one's demise

Fortunately I'm not a crustacean
Forcibly yanked from the sea
I'm merely a girl with a viral complaint
Not viewed as a delicacy

Thus I should quit whining
And focus on being ill
For my head in the freezer could I stick
And with the frozen peas chill.

Atchoo

Can't stop sneezing
Coughing and wheezing

Can't stop blowing
Nose is running and glowing

Can't stop sweating
Fever's well and truly set in

Can't stop aching
Feels like my head is breaking

Burning up
Confined to my bed

Soggy tissues
Filled with gunk from my head

TV's on
But it's painful to watch

Sleep eludes me
'Cause I keep waking up

I lie in bed
And wait for it to pass

No appetite
Just fluids en masse

Paracetamols
A hot toddy here and there

Whiskey, lemon, honey
Is all that I can bear

Flat on my back
Until I've won the fight

Just got to surrender
When you're feeling this sh*te.

Back In The Flow

Excitement bubbling deep within
A plan finally coming together
Sounds that have been dormant
Vibrating 'neath the surface
Breaking through the storms I've weathered

No longer shall I be silenced
I have rhythms to create
And words to put to music
For it's never too late

The wheels are in motion
Dreams to be realised
Awakening from their slumber
And aspirations revitalised

Each day I take steps
To bring them to life
Dates in the diary
Ideas rife

Excitement building
A swelling tide
Bursting at the seems
I'm braced for the ride

A waterfall
Cascading down
The heavens having opened
Ideas abound

The cosmic flow
Depositing opportunities at my door
I grasp them all
I am blocked no more.

Backhanded Victory

Went to return a phone
It didn't have a loud speaker

Dealt with the proprietor
An extremely abrasive geezer

Blood rushed to his head
For I didn't have the box

They'd kept it at point of sale
It wasn't actually lost

When I requested a refund
He THREW me out of the shop!

Called me a 'Silly B*tch'
As he pelted me with the dosh...

Barren

Dry as the desert
Underneath the setting sun
I yearn for you to shower me
With a torrent of love

Scattered am I
Infinite grains of sand
Oh, for you to scoop me up
In your strong and tender hands

I see you on the horizon
Or are you just a mirage?
Will you vanish if I approach?
Out of reach, always at large?

Be Kind

Yesterday
Another soul gave up
Departed this life
For she'd endured enough

She couldn't take
This world anymore
So she took flight
From behind closed doors

We'll never know
The final trigger
But something snapped
Something she just couldn't figure

A way out from
No apparent escape
The only option
Her own life to take

The outpouring of grief
We now see
The abundance of love
Is a tragedy

For she'll never feel it
Too little too late
The odds were stacked against
This vilified victim of hate

I didn't know her
But her death resonates
In bleaker times
Have I contemplated such a fate

But I never had to contend
With the added pressure
Of overwhelming scrutiny
And being tabloid fodder

Whatever took place
On that December day
Should not have ended
In this utterly heartbreaking way

That a tormented young woman
Had to kill herself
For people to finally realise
How badly she needed help

To deal with a world
That had seemingly turned its back
Upon the beautiful but broken star
We knew as Caroline Flack.

Beggars Belief

Ain't too proud to beg
Pays more than a regular job
With wages so low
And nowhere to go
It's hard to blame this baying mob

At every turn
An outstretched hand
A fee for everything
As they approach and demand

A career of sorts
Professionals are they
As they show you a 'kindness'
Or deliberately lead you astray

Then hit you up
At an extortionate rate
Though sympathetic to their plight
You start to hate

This insatiable hunger
They feel inside
As you see the pound signs
Flashing before their eyes

When a visitor passes by
'A walking ATM'
Perceived to be full of cash
To be emptied out by them

On you like a plague
They'll quickly rinse you clean
If you don't have your wits about you
If you're generous instead of mean

An impossible situation
It really wears you down
Caught in a full-blown tourist trap
Ravenous they hound

Concentrated at every site
The beggars lie in wait
Harass you with all their might
Until you're in an exasperated state

And if you don't cough up
They'll spit at you or curse
Or threaten to beat you up
That's a fact – could it get any worse?

These parasites that swarm
Around the city of Marrakech
Are a horrific blight on a place
I so wanted me to impress

The way they aggressively prey
On the travellers that flow
Sadly ruined what I truly hoped would be
A magical place to go.

Beings Of Light

Little beings of light
Appeared in my mind's eye
Electrifying were they
I couldn't help but cry

Angels, I believe
That came when I called them in
To affirm that they were real
Not a figment existing therein

So bright they blinded me
Fluttering were their wings
A gift right there to see
My heart began to sing.

Big Up Or Shut Up

Spread love not hate
Celebrate
Each other's success
Share the happiness

Don't cast a dark shadow
When someone else is doing well
Be supportive
Not jealous as hell

We all deserve
The good things in life
A sprinkling of stardust
Should be everyone's right

If people bring you down
When you are on the up
They clearly don't deserve you
It's so messed up

The green-eyed monster
Should not prevail
Don't stand for its antics
Turn on your tail

If your tribe can't provide you
With a genuine smile
When you're proud of an achievement
Then run a mile

Life can be tough
Solidarity should be sought
Not rivalry, one-upmanship
And negative retorts

Surround yourself
With your biggest fans
The ones on your wavelength
Who'll shake your hand

The ones who've got your back
Through thick and thin
Who big you up
And want you to win

Those who'll help lift you
When you reach for the skies
Who won't be staring daggers
From behind envious green eyes.

Blueberry Crush

Shades of magenta
Violet and blue
My wrist has taken on
A psychedelic hue

Underneath
The translucent skin
Aquamarine
And yellow flecks mixed in

All colours of the spectrum
Adorn my lower arm
Like having a tattoo
That bleeds into my palm

Which echoes the scheme
As colours blend with veins
Even there
Trickles the purple rain.

Blue January

The bleak side of Christmas
January blues
Finances pinched
Tax returns loom

A lack of sun
Everything grey
Long, dark nights,
Freezing, soggy days

Winter lurgies
Harsh and unpleasant
Bugs, colds, flu
Honey and lemon

Sweating buckets
Lying in bed
Shivers and tingles
Banging heads

Drinking fluids
Fortified soups
Daytime TV
Endless soaps

Time off work
But no fun to be had
Vegetating profusely
Feeling wretched, beyond bad

New Year's resolutions
Of keeping fit
Parked for now
Until we no longer feel s**t

Roll on February
And the elusive Valentine
Who'll send us roses
And ply us with wine

Smother us in chocolate
And lick it all off
We can but dream –
As we sneeze, splutter and cough!

Bladders That Go Bump In The Night

When nature calls
Thou must obey
Except when in slumber
That just isn't OK

Suddenly you wake
And wonder why
Until you hear
Your bladder cry

The sensation creeps in
Building in strength
You try to ignore it
But it won't relent

You turn and twist
Willing it to subside
But a swell is building
Between your thighs

With the dam about to burst
You yank yourself up
Leg it to the loo
Entreating the urge to stop

'Til you're safely in the bathroom
And can finally let go
Bleary-eyed yet relieved
As you allow your pee to flow

But your problems aren't over yet
Here's where the real challenge comes
Will you ever get back to sleep?
Now your bladder has banged its drum?

It's 5am
Dawn has started to break
You're no longer in pain
But you're wide awake!

And no amount of counting sheep
Can knock you out again
And so you curse your bladder
For depriving of sleep your brain

You lie there staring at the ceiling
Lamenting your bad luck
Conclude you must admit defeat
And reluctantly get up.
Way too early.

Breaking Away

When being with someone
Makes you feel more alone
It's obvious something's wrong
And the connection is gone

When someone doesn't value your presence
Whilst you are physically there
It's hard to take but you must make that break
And leave because they clearly don't care

You are worthy of their undivided attention
It should really be a given
There's no point in wasting your precious time
It may be hard but it's the right decision

So cut your losses and walk away
Go where you're wanted and welcome
Cut the tie that causes pain
Do it for self-preservation

Don't be a glutton for punishment
Caught in a vicious circle
It's madness to expect a different outcome
And will only lead to torture infernal

Don't be made to feel invisible
Rise up, step into your power
Don't allow your voice to be ignored
Stand tall and as proud as a tower

Don't ever be taken for granted
Or driven to the end of your tether
Be fearless and seek pastures new
Knowing that you deserve better.

Broken Spell

Broken spell
Heart intact
A blessed release
To my senses back

The shackles are off
I rise again
Consigned to history
Are you, my 'friend'.

Bubble Gum

Bubble gum is amazing
It stretches when you blow
You can wrap it miles around your tongue
And inflate that stuff like dough

Especially Hubba Bubba
The stretchiest of them all
Blow that mutha f***er
And you can have a ball!

But remember it's only membrane
Though tough it has its limits
It'll only stretch so far
'Til it splits and covers you in it

Stretchy things aren't infinite
Even they can be spread too thin
So careful with that stuff
Or it'll burst and splat, done in.

The same applies to people
They can only bend so far
Before they inevitably snap
Broken, clean in half.

We only have one pair of hands
And helpful as one can be
If everyone wants a piece of you
It becomes an impossibility

To fulfil their needs
And still meet your own
You end up depleted
Clapped out, on the floor

So you must set boundaries
Look after yourself
Learn to say 'no'
Think of your health

When it all gets too much
That's a red flag right there
So take a step back
Regroup and take care

For if you're burnt out
You're no good to anyone
So repeat after me:
"I'm not a piece of bubblegum."

Bubblicious

Loving life in lockdown
Living in my bubble
Listening to my favourite music
Shielded from life's struggles

Writing to my heart's content
Strumming my guitar
The outside world seems miles away
I'm looking at the stars

Long may it continue
Who needs reality?
When in my little dreamworld
I feel completely free

Time to get creative
Time to get things done
Time now for myself
Banging my own drum

Dancing to my own tune
Productivity maximised
Creating a new future
Reaching for the skies

Ready for new horizons
When this thing is over
Off to pastures new
Without stress upon my shoulders

A new cycle is beginning
The old one playing out
My future's in safe hands
Of that I'm in no doubt.

Butterflies...

He moved me but
He didn't know
We were on the cusp
The feelings began to flow

I felt drawn to him
And was willing to merge
But we were interrupted
And our little bubble burst

And so he left
Went back to his life
But the impression he made
Has caused me some strife

This lost opportunity
May never come again
Though I yearn for him
But he won't relent

So I bottle it up
Keep it locked inside
But when I think of him
Butterflies arise

In the pit of my stomach
Fluttering away
And then he infiltrates my dreams
So that when I awake

I'm aching for him
Wishing he was nearby
But we are far apart
Though these emotions won't subside

What to do?
Powerless it seems
The one that got away
If only he knew how much he means.

Camel Capers

If you should mount a camel
Brace yourself for bumps
It may make you squeal in terror
As it hoists itself up with a jump

Ensure that you lean back
Or you'll lurch forward arse over tit
There's a technique to this camel lark
And I'm yet to master it!

Once you're up
You feel relatively safe
Until it starts moving
And gathers pace

Negotiating the sand dunes
Is no mean feat
It's fine going up
But coming down your butt flies off the seat

You cling on for dear life
As you bounce like a ping-pong ball
Akin to riding rodeo
Trying desperately not to fall

Grappling with a camel
Is something of an art
They seem so cute and calm
Until they snort and fart

Until they get the 'hump'
And threaten to throw you off
Be very kind to your camel
You're doomed if you make it cross!

Your palms will sweat
And slip from the handle
Calluses will develop
As you ride this risky ramble

Your biceps will bulge
And your abs will take a beating
Your bum will be raw like a baboon's arse
And way too sore for seating

Getting off it you're still in peril
And take your life in your hands
As its front legs buckle beneath you
Almost hoying you head first into the sand

You'll struggle to walk
With wobbly jelly legs
And you'll be straddling around
Like you've been rogered by King Dong and his friends

Your back will seriously ache
But you'll be eternally thankful to be alive
So hail one of these creatures with caution
As it's one hell of a white-knuckle ride!

Carbonated

Don't you burst my bubble
Or rain on my parade
I'm walking on sunshine
Not stepping in your shade

I am on a high
Things are going fine
Got a spring in my step
And I'm feeling divine

Join me if you want to
But do not bring me down
Had enough of negativity
And never will I drown

Firing on all cylinders
Bursting with energy
Feeling light and zingy
Effervescent and carefree

As if I could actually fly
To the magical end of a rainbow
On the wings of a unicorn
Wafting which way the wind blows

Through iridescent, turquoise skies
And fluffy cappuccino clouds
Dodging dancing golden rays
That glisten all around

This vibe is sublime
I'm not causing any trouble
So stay out of my way
I won't let you burst my bubble.

Chords

Time to let go
But finding it hard
Strings are tugging
At my heart

When you've been tied to someone
For so long
And you need to walk away
You have to be strong

Seems an impossible task
Willpower non-existent
Head telling you the right thing to do
Emotions pulling you in the opposite direction

How do you switch it off?
When someone is under your skin?
Coursing through your veins?
Not physically here but within?

It only took a moment
To undo all that hard work
Progress that had been made
Discarded, cast away, shirked

Now to begin again
Building up that wall
Encasing those feelings in an iron coffin
Burying it deep beneath, in a vault

Forgetting all over again
How it was when it was great
Trying to only focus
On the bad times and the hate

But how can you focus on the hate?
When all there really is is love?
When seeing them again takes your breath away?
When you're insanely thinking you can never have enough?

Cursed I am it seems
Afflicted by that which has no cure
I just wish he'd spared me this
Never returned to these helpless shores

Who knows how long I will toil
And writhe in this agony
Until blessed numbness sets in
And once again I am free.

Clarification

You may not know where I'm coming from
You may not know where I've been
I may not be good at expressing myself
You may not always know what I mean

I'll try to put into words
Exactly what I'm trying to convey
But if you struggle to understand me
Don't jump to conclusions – just say!

Ask me for elucidation
To expand on the point I have made
And I will endeavour to illustrate
That thought which is inside my brain

I may illustrate this with pictures
Or perhaps I will sing you a song
You may have to peel back some layers
If so, please do it with compassion

I may do this with intonation
So pay attention to the tone of my voice
Sometimes I may not be able to verbalise
What I'm feeling but please realise

That I'm doing my very best
To communicate clearly to you all
If I flounder at times be patient
Especially if I should stall

For words have a plethora of meanings
And contexts they can be placed in
If we misunderstand each other at times
Issues may arise herein

So listen with ears wide open
Never assume you know
Don't interrupt when someone is speaking
You may just spoil their flow

This is the way we should interact
To formulate a strong foundation
For not everything is always crystal clear
Sometimes we require clarification.

Crucifying Crutches

Foot crocked
They issued crutches
Two great sticks
Made of metal and plastic

To help her walk
Or hinder, as was the case,
For she couldn't quite carry
Her own body weight

So off she hobbled
From A&E
Her arms in braces
The crutches roaming free

But it quickly became apparent
That she needed superhuman strength
To power down the street
On one leg, the other bent

If only she'd known
She could've pre-trained at the gym
Built up some biceps
Got some guns going on

Alas, she hadn't an inkling
This was out of the blue
Blue being the colour
Her swollen palms now had a hue

As bruises developed
And calluses formed
From pushing down
On rock-hard handles that burned

And try carrying a bag
Or picking up shopping
Whilst brandishing crutches
And flaming hopping!

An impossible feat
With one foot in pain
Never mind trying not skid over
When it started to rain!

And then the momentous
Task of negotiating stairs
Gazing upwards from the bottom
Trying not to burst into tears

Should she crawl on her knees
Like a toddler, on all fours?
Could she afford to have a stairlift
Quickly installed?

And how to get down
Once up and scared of heights?
Without a parachute
Oh, f**k, Jesus Christ!

So the bum-shuffle it is
One step at a time
Whilst somehow holding crutches
And not catapulting herself and flying!

WHY did she elect
To live in the attic?
Three floors above a shop
No lift, how tragic!

Had she predicted
She would be in this plight
She would never have chosen
To dwell virtually in the sky!

But, alas, it was tough titties
This was exactly the case
So she had to soldier on
And ultimately embrace

The sad status quo:
"Come on, girl, you got this!
"Do not be defeated
"By crucifying crutches!"

Cupid's Bow

Speak from the heart
With eyes open wide
Then when Cupid fires his arrow
Your message its target will find

The words won't get lost in translation
When you shoot with his beautiful bow
And you'll pierce the heart of they upon whom
You want your love to bestow.

DD-Cup Cakes

The lemon muffins on display
In Starbucks are quite rude
Positioned in pairs, with pointed iced tips
They look suspiciously like boobs

Turned over on their sides
Full and bursting out
They immediately caught my eye
And made me laugh out loud

Like bulging bosoms
Veritable sugar 'tits'
I actually cracked a smile
And almost lost my s**t!

What cheeky little chappy
Was the author of this joke?
That brightened up my morning
As I trudged to work in the snow?

He must be a breast man
Bazookas his weakness
Harbouring an obsession
With the female chest

To liken them to muffins
Is actually quite strange
Perhaps he's fixated with Mary's Berries
From her Bake-Off days

Or maybe it's simply just
My own silly, warped mind
That associates muffins with mammaries
Because there're two turned on their sides

Who knows, but it tickled me pink
And I totally had to share
For the sight of them made me happy
So forgive me for going there...

Defused & Confused

Fuse lit
She began to smoulder
Sizzling, burning
Tingling all over

A raging furnace
Was ignited
At last alive
Infused, excited

He continued to pour
Fuel on the fire
The flames increased
Climbing higher and higher

They touched the sky
Setting it ablaze
Common sense incinerated
She succumbed in a daze

Then all at once
A power cut
She felt herself shrinking
As he pulled the plug

Plummeting now
Back down to Earth
She crash-landed
And it really hurt

Disposable
As toilet paper
Flushed away
Without a 'see you later!'

A hazardous encounter
She really didn't need
Although she licked her wounds
They continued to bleed

That she could be treated
In this way
Illustrates the sickening culture
Pervading 'dating' today

A veritable minefield
Where one is dehumanised
Picked up and then put down
Blown out, cast aside

The instant gratification
Of communicating online
Negates the need it seems
To meet up in real life

A first 'date' can be had
Using video call
You get the general gist
Having made barely any effort at all

And before you know it
You've been virtually 'banged'
Used to scratch an itch
'Wham, bam, thank you, m'am!'

They then disappear
To wreak havoc elsewhere
Leaving you out in the cold
Stranded, up in the air

Virtual ratbags
Who you can't even slap
Who hide behind screens
Dishing out their crap

Cowardly pussies
Not lions in this case
Who don't have the gumption
To meet face-to-face

So impersonal
Heartless as hell
More evidence of zombification
Devoid of emotion as well

Distinctly soulless
Operating like machines
By remote control
Riding roughshod over feelings

Immune to the fact
There's an actual person somewhere
Who might be upset
By this lack of care

So the radio silence
Was deafening
She vowed never again
To be so sucked in

She chalked it up
To experience
Rebuilt her walls
The first line of defence

As for online dating
And scraping the bottom of the well:
F**k swiping left and right
It can go to hell.

Diary Of The Disconnected

What a palaver
When your account's been slammed
No internet or landline
Communications jammed

Who's to blame?
Plusnet/Skye/EE?
All say "No!
It wasn't me!"

So while they pass me
From pillar to post
I report them to OFFCOM
Now surely they're toast!

Can't cut me off
For two whole weeks
And expect me to roll over
And turn the other cheek

I've been stitched up
Through no fault of my own
Wi-Fi is no more
Running through my home

So I sit and I wait
Under house arrest
From the crack of dawn 'til noon
At their inconvenient behest

For an engineer to appear
And rectify my plight
Get me back online
Before I lose my sh*te

He's cutting it really fine
This elusive man from BT
Another telecoms company
To add to the other three

You'd think between the four of them
They could sort this major mess out
Not condemn me to more complaining
And shooting off my mouth

I've already had to take
A whole day off of work
Pay to use a net café
And it's driving me berserk

Buy some extra data
So I can surf at least from my phone
And now I am a prisoner
A jailbird having a moan

Fast forward now an hour
The swine did not show up
Called Plusnet yet again
And spoke to some other dumb f**k

Who told me my order was cancelled
By Orange – what a joke!
Another corporation to add to the mix
Now that's five I want up in smoke

She then changed her tune
After putting me on hold
For an interminable time
As my blood boiled with these woes

"Oh, sorry, he came at nine
And fixed things externally"
A day off work was not required
Well thanks for telling me!

Incandescent I tear into her ear
Wishing I could pinch her face
If only this rep of Plusnet were here
What a balls-up, an utter disgrace!

"Yes, it's unfortunate."
Understatement of the year
I'm seething at this heartless t**t

Who unfortunately doesn't
Empathise
And is only increasing my wrath

So I ask for the boss
To lodge a complaint
I'm that flaming angry
I could actually faint

I must wait for a call
As he's not around
Typical, I think
What a bunch of clowns

I'll update again
When I have more news
Until then must I simmer
As my screws are now loose.

Divine Timing

Timing is everything
It's important to get it right
But sometimes we have no control
Over what happens in our lives

When I was taking some time
Things spiralled out of control
A series of events
Sparked something to unfold

Which ultimately set me free
A blessing in disguise
And now the dust has settled
I see with clearer eyes

It had to happen this way
For it was taken out of my hands
I didn't need to act
For God did have a plan

And now I have what I wished for
I can move forward with my life
For He is in control
And no more shall there be strife

And His timing is always
Perfect without a doubt
He knows what He is doing
So don't question the ins and outs

Just trust that all is well
When He is at the helm
And then sit back and relax
And be at peace within your realm.

Drunken Easter Bleatings

Rachel Rhodes
Aka The Poisonous Pixie
I like to kick butt
When I'm feeling verbally frisky

I churn out a poem
Put the world to rights
Some of you may feel
I'm talking utter sh*te

But I don't really care
For my need to express is rife
Can't bottle up your opinions
You've only got one life

I spend my days
In the 9-5
Dreaming of bigger things
A better life

So I'll keep writing
In the lyrical fashion
Until I'm winning
Getting a piece of the action

I've got plans
No time to waste
While the sun shines
I'm making hay

Got me a lover
And a possee of friends
Don't need much more
Until the fantasy begins!

Ecstasy

It comes in waves
Tingling all over me
Burning at the centre
Permeating outwards
I convulse with pleasure
Breaking into a sweat
Experiencing sheer bliss
For that one moment in time
I reach for the heavens
And burst into a billion stars.

Escape

A brand-new day is born
The sun has now arisen
Who knows what's to come
In this perception prism

Light refracted this way and that
People intermingling through it
Riffing off each other as they go
Their inner worlds reacting to it

Nature the observer to it all
A tree quietly poised in the ground
Tranquil and noble it stands tall
And doesn't make a sound

The bustling city alive with noise
Money to be made
How I yearn to leave it all behind
And return to my sacred place.

Eye On You

I feel your vibe
Instinct tells me
Something inside
That you could want me

The chemistry burns
Well, I'm ready when you are
You don't have to yearn
You've already come this far

I'm waiting for you
You're wasting my time
You silly fool
Come and be mine.

Fever Pitch

Panic stations all around
Bog roll's flying off the shelves
Coronavirus is London-bound
As en masse we sanitise ourselves

Lockdown could be coming
So grab your pasta and baked beans
Bulk buy as much grub as you can
Loot and ransack the likes of Sainsbury's

Cause a riot
Jump the queue
It's round the block
No waiting in line for you!

Stockpile everything
Then batten down the hatches
Binge on the paranoia
The media's fuelling in massive batches

The world's gone mad
A pandemic of insanity
As everyone starts self-isolating
Instead of roaming free

What to think?
Who to believe?
Is this real?
Or a conspiracy?!

Is it a bid?
To cull the population?
Is germ warfare at hand?
Or truly an accident of nature?

It's hard to ascertain
Who the good guys are in this
Some say it's a stunt to privatise
Our beloved NHS

Europe, we know,
Isn't taking any chances
But brazen Blighty
Has yet to act to contain the advances

Of the virus
(If indeed it's as bad as they say)
Which makes me wonder WTF
Is being kept from the public domain?

What does Boris know?
That the rest of the world does not?
Or does our government genuinely not care
If half of us pop our clogs?

I didn't vote them in
Never trusted them anyway
And now I dislike them even more
For we're sitting ducks here in the UK

But not to worry
If our liberty IS being revoked
As long as we can wipe our bums
We won't care if we're not in on the 'joke'

For in all this hysteria
Those still 'asleep'
Will listen to the hype
Until it's too late to weep

Over the fact that the prophetic
Novel *Nineteen Eighty-Four*
Could soon be our reality
Now common sense is out the door.

Fifth November

November fifth
Is soon to come
Explosions of colour
And gunpowder fun

The Guy on the bonfire
Awaits incineration
Toffee apples, candy floss
There for our delectation

Dark winter nights
Are now pulling in
Be sure to wrap up warm
To see Fawkes night in.

First Love

First love
Where it all began

First everything
More than holding hands

First sleep
Curled up as one

First dawn
Awakening to greet the sun

First heartbreak
Deeper than the rest

Torrential tears
Because I loved you the best.

Flakes

Flaky people
Can get on your wick
They let others down
Perhaps for kicks

It seems they're more important
Than everybody else
That the world revolves around them
So absorbed are they in themselves

Don't be at the mercy of flakes
Value your own time more!
It's just as precious as theirs
More so because it's yours

Don't let flakes mess you around
Ditch those that do offend
Only the reliable ones
Deserve to be your friend.

Flower Power

It's Poppy Day
We commemorate the bloodshed
Tides of crimson petals
A nod to the many dead

100 years
Since the First World War
And what have we learnt?
What was it all for?

For we did it all again
In 1939
And I see no glory in either
Just a massive waste of life

War is not the answer
I believe in peace
Sending innocent people off to die
Should be a crime I feel

How can murder be justified?
And on such an enormous scale?
Where is the honour in that?
For me words almost fail

If we refuse to be used in this way
Refuse to pick up arms
Who would fight the politician's wars?
Who would come to harm?

Surely if we stand together
The many would outnumber the few
We shouldn't be made to fight
If we actually don't want to

My heart goes out to the fallen
And, yes, we should remember their names
For they paid the ultimate price
For being lured into someone else's sick game

But I will not wear a poppy
The symbol of a bullet wound
I do not wish to appear as if shot
Blood gushing as I meet my doom

I cannot abide violence
In any shape or form
So I choose not to wear this flower on this day
Or a hypocrite I'd become.

For Lucas

Dearest Lucas
You bundle of scrum
It's darling to meet you
I hope we'll be chums

You're all soft and squidgy
And minuscule
You smell like buttermilk
And make us all drool

I held you tonight
And fell in love
You melted my heart
And made it thud

My first GREAT nephew
Offspring of Mush
The initial nephew
Who was also cute and lush

Just in time for Christmas
Oh what a gift
A gurgling, bouncing baby
Who could resist?

The charm of 'Little Legs'
And what he'll become
As he embarks on his life
Guided by his dad and mum

I think you are awesome
So welcome to the fold
Even if it makes me
Feel really old!

I'm still glad you're here
And that is a fact
So much love and snuggles
Your Great-aunt Rach.

F**k With Me Not!

That wonderful feeling
When you finally snap
After tolerating bullsh*t
For so long you hit back

You take it on the chin
As much as you can bear
For the sake of a peaceful life
Duping t**ts into thinking you're scared

When in actual fact
You simply choose your battles
Discerningly
Even though you may be rattled

For you've better things to do
Than rise to childish bate
You're a hippy and a lover
And opt not to participate

However there is a limit
And eventually you blow
Come out with all guns blazing
Your true warrior colours on show

A force to be reckoned with
No shrinking violet are you
When you're on a mission
There is no stopping you

So beware the little Hitlers
And one-upmanship brigade
Beware those who take the p*ss
And those who would have you enslaved

You have a right to be here
And deserve a level of respect
You're not a f**king number
Or a machine that fulfils requests

You're a beautifully complex
Human being
With your own crap to deal with
And a life to lead

You shouldn't have to apologise
Beg, borrow or steal
You shouldn't have to bow down to others
Who feel they reign supreme

We all should be treated as equals
The hierarchy defunct and abolished
No one is better than anyone else
And such thoughts therein demolished

We're all born, we all die
And we all need to sh*t
We all look the same naked
So deal with it

Money, rank
And birth shouldn't matter
And if you believe it does
You're as mad as a hatter

If you're on this planet
And live and breathe
You're worth your weight in gold
So don't f**king mess with me.

Gratitude

The calm after the storm
What is rightfully mine returned
Peace of mind restored
Necessary bridges burned

The threat to my security
Dealt with by the law
Fraudulent activity
Finally is no more

The burden has been lifted
That had weighed me down so
Free at last from anguish
An opportunity now for growth

I thank my Higher Power
For whispering in my ear
Illuminating my path
When I was crippled with fear

I thank the Universe
For breaking me out of 'jail'
For I had done my time
And justice has prevailed

I thank the Fellowship
For curing me of my disease
For steering me through the storm
When I was on my knees

God does certainly work
In mysterious ways
And He will clear all obstacles
With His amazing grace

Courage can sometimes fail you
Anxiety can eat you up
But if you have Faith inside you
You will never be stuck.

F**king Adverts!

Adverts, adverts, adverts
I royally detest
Non-subliminal brain-washing
Of the masses – I protest!

Telling me what to buy
Vacuuming up my cash
Greedy, guzzling commercials
Horrible, stupid trash

Every couple of minutes
On most TV stations
They churn them out incessantly
For every conceivable occasion

Making out I need
The sh*te they're trying to flog
And if the product is dull
It'll be accompanied by a cute dog

Or a half-naked woman
Who's impossibly beautiful
Or a chiselled, ripped young man
Semi-clad and in a thong

Even food is sexyfied
With a voiceover akin to Je T'Aime
And it's OK if I swerve it
For they'll repeat it over and over again

Until it's ringing in my ears
And I'm singing it in my sleep
Until I can't even bear to watch
And the jingle makes me howl and weep

Until I've lost the will to live
And have scratched out both my eyes
Or until I've hurled my TV out
Of the window and seen it fly

These adverts make me seethe
They're on longer than the programme itself
And if you want to continue watching
You're condemned to enduring them as well

So I seldom switch the thing on
For mostly it's a box of crap
A vehicle for peddling junk
And quite frankly I can do without that.

Geronimo...

The theatre beckons
A stage of a kind
Though anaesthetised
I'm the 'star' if you like

With morphine dancing
Through my veins
I'll be oblivious, hopefully
To the pain

Under the knife
Spark out cold
I'll put my faith in God
That I make it home

Only six months ago
Was I in this scenario
Never expected an encore
And to have to undergo

This experience again
Let alone so soon
Can't I please abstain?
Be spared the surgeon's tool?

"Nay," said he,
"It must come out!
"We mustn't waste time!
"Mustn't dither about!"

So when tomorrow comes
On a gurney will I be
In thick, white spandex tights,
A backless gown and asleep

I won't deny I'm scared
I'm bricking it in actual fact
I recall it's like facing the gallows
You fear you're not coming back

Yet needs must I suppose
So I'll try hard to 'man up'
That said, if you are inclined
Say a wee prayer and wish me luck?!

Gone – With The Wind

Good evening everyone
From the bottom of my heart
But pardon me
If I happen to fart!

Only yesterday
I had a colonic
And ever since it happened
I've been trumping something chronic

Apparently this treatment
Is the answer to my prayers
Aside from the fact
It brought to my eyes tears

A jet wash was inserted
Deep into my rear
And then my arse was lambasted
With water which was queer

A very odd sensation
Uncomfortable too
Like whitewater rapids
Are raging inside of you

In did it pour
'Til I was quite inflated
It seriously gave me cramps
I felt far from constipated

The opposite in fact
Was the desired effect
And intermittently
Did I begin to detect

Through the looking glass
That was trained on the tube
Protruding from my rectum
Little bits of poop

Floating away
Into the abyss
I didn't know how to feel
Other than physically sick

But apparently this was good
And now internally I was cleansed!
I prayed it was over
But she repeated it again

This time using a concoction
Of liquid and herbs
Like I was a teapot
Brewing something hideous

And lo and behold
What goes up must come down
And once again I passed
Lots of stuff that was brown

Duped was I into thinking
That that was quite enough
But it wasn't over yet
For she had to pull the plug

And remove the hose pipe
Once and for all
Basically unleashing
Niagara Falls!

I just about had time
To leg it to the salle de bain
Before the heavens opened
And a torrent engulfed the can

Now I know what inspired
The phrase 'to have the squits'
I squitted for half an hour
I must have been full of it!

Whence it all came
I will never know
But apparently I'll need
Another session in a week or so

And then my tummy
Again will be flat
I'll lose two stone at least
And diamonds will be shat

For I've been purified
From the inside out
It cost me a fortune
But my bowels are in no doubt

That they are pristine
And gleaming like the sun
Which I can now with conviction say
Shines right out of my bum!

Grief

The pain that we feel
When the showers come
Is born from the gift
Of having loved someone

And even though they've transitioned
To another plane
That love keeps us connected
Until we meet again

Until then let the angels
Lend you their wings
And cradle you from underneath
Forming a lifeboat that sings.

Hello Sunshine!

Run into the sun
As fast as you can
Catch it while it's there
You know you want to run

High in the sky
Shining so bright
Lighting up the world
Putting wrongs to right

Where were you hiding –
You took so long to rise?
Now here you are
Right before my eyes

Golden and hot
Your rays beam down on me
Warming my skin
Winter a memory

We all come alive
And feel our spirits lift
Out in the fresh air
To be a part of it

Summer now dawns
Get ready to partay
We've waited so long
To feel this heavenly way.

Hot Air

Blowing hot air
You rant and you rage
A torrent of pain
As you vent and rampage

A bark but also a bite
Each as bad as the other
Your spew it all out at once
As your victims quiver and shudder

No apparent end in sight
The regime stands ever tall
How 'big' of you, Mr,
To make others feel small.

Hugs

During this pandemic
I'm stockpiling hugs
And when it's all over
I'm pulling the plug

And unleashing the lot
On all I hold dear
Those far and wide
I yearn to be near

My heart is brimming
Full of hugs
For those that I care about
And Jesus it's tough

But they won't go to waste
They're just getting stronger
I've got so many to give
I can wait a little longer

So I'm hoarding those hugs
And making a list
Of everyone upon whom
I'm going to inflict

The hug of the millennium
So that these people know
How much I genuinely care
And how much I've missed them so

I don't care if I hug them
Within an inch of their lives
I'm going to hug them so hard
They never have to think twice

About how much they mean
To little old me
And how much it hurts
When them I can't see

Physical human contact
When forbidden is craved
We shouldn't take it for granted
Ever again

To shake someone's hand
Or give them a kiss
Is a priceless privilege
A precious gift

We all need cuddles
To keep us alive
A pair of comforting arms around us
From time to time

And that time will come
Eventually
So I'm stockpiling hugs
Until I can set them all free.

Humbled Thanks

If you're reading this forgive me
If I've appeared weak
If I've displayed my hurt
And anger whilst feeling bleak

Been to hell and back
Through the mincing machine
Now trying to get my life back on track
And wipe that filthy slate clean

Still processing so much
Feeling fragile so to speak
But the worst is over now
And peace of mind do I seek

Wrung out, overtired
I search for inner strength
Seems I've forgotten how to pray
Yet am desperate to reconnect

The thunderstorm has passed
And vindicated have I been
Bathed in compassion
Most unexpectedly

Yes, the earthquake hit
But the cavalry arrived
It's now the aftershocks
That I hope will soon subside

And though I'm on shaky ground
I know who's got my back
And these angels have lifted me up
Shielded me from attack

All along I was protected
Although I didn't know
I've had to face some of my worst fears
But hopefully I will grow

Thank you to all
Who've been there for me
I'm filled with gratitude
So overwhelmed I can barely speak.

Ice Maiden

Like a frozen waterfall
The tears in my eyes crystallise
My bleeding heart stops beating
And slowly turns to ice

The blood in my veins runs cold
My skin has a deathly blue hue
A glacier I have become
An iceberg, because of you

A white island adrift on the ocean
To sink you if you draw too close
Sharp edges to rip you apart
Ask *Titanic* for she doth know.

It's Never Too Late

Today a dream
I dreamed came true
A promise I made
To myself that I'd do

A lifetime ago
I was only eighteen
But I knew back then
One day it would be real

The road's been long
And at times beyond tough
But I held on to that vision
And I never gave up

I dealt with the doubters
The haters and thieves
Those out to get me
Through jealousy and greed

I faltered for a while
But now I've made it back
Against the odds
And that is that

Thanks be to God
And the universe
For giving me the keys
To finally lift the curse.

Just Wanted To Say...

Seasons greetings to everyone
On this Christmas Eve
The big day is only a sleep away
And I hope that you find peace

That you share it with loved ones
Or very dear friends
And take pleasure in the gifts you receive

That you eat and drink
Delicious food
Surrounded by sparkly things

I'm lighting candles and saying prayers
That those I care for are well
I'm thankful for the little things
That we cannot buy or sell

I hope that love flows
Through everyone's hearts
And that wishes you make come true

That happiness reigns
Throughout the coming year
And you enjoy what is best for you

So Merry Christmas
And blessings galore
Whether you're near or far

Let this time
Bring out the best in you
And those you hold close to your hearts.

Labour Of Love

'Twas the day of the election
And all was insane
Boris actually hid in a fridge
Dodging interviews again

He stood up Radio 2
Upsetting not just Jeremy Vine
His flunky swore on live TV
Yesterday morning at breakfast time

Can't say I'd appreciate him
Delivering my milk
Wouldn't want it to curdle
From being exposed to someone of his ilk

Corbyn, on the other hand
Is rapidly showing himself to be
By and large the better man
Wanting to improve lives for the many

So think very carefully
Before you cast your votes
The Tories have cocked up everything
Maybe Labour should have a go

Don't normally do
Actual politics
But this year I'd really love
To boot out all the pricks

Who don't give a damn
About the likes of us
Who are struggling to get by
And working off our nuts

The country's in dire straits
I fear for the NHS
I'm sickened by the sight
Of increasing homelessness

I'm furious that the rich
Are in the minority
Yet they hold all the cards
And all the power and money

We all deserve to live
Not exist hand-to-mouth
If wealth was distributed evenly
This mess could be sorted out

Share and share alike
That's what I was taught
Greed is one of the deadly sins
But some their riches hoard

So vote for each other
Not just for yourselves
Vote for a better future
So that everyone does well

The Messiah isn't coming
So let's be our own saviour
And on this Election Day
FFS please vote Labour!
#jeremycorbyn #generalelection

Lost At Sea?

My ship is sinking
Going down
Trouble and strife
Me surrounds

I stand alone
As water floods in
My bow is breaking
The waves are too big

Is it self-destruction
Or being a victim of circumstance?
What does it even matter?
Pretty soon I'll be sank

Food for the fishes
Lying on the sea bed
In my watery grave
Yay, perhaps better off when dead

I surrender to the tide
Can't fight this anymore
Been treading water for way too long
Now tired drown I for sure

So long my friends
And lovers past
Au revoir family
Guess I wasn't built to last

I'd say it's been a hoot
But right now I feel defeat
Maybe on the day of reckoning
I'll see it differently

Until then I shall close my eyes
Inhale the salt water in
Praying that I rest in peace
When in my liquid coffin.

Love

Love is the sweetest thing
Love's tail can have a sting
Love doesn't always stay
Love can change every day

Love has many different guises
Love is unpredictable, full of surprises
Love can come from different sources
People, animals, unseen forces

Love is a feeling
Love is an act
Love can be physical
Love can be lacked

Love can be rejected
Love can be withheld
Love can make us crazy
Love can be unrequited as well

Love can be offered
Love can be sought
But love is not a commodity
That can be sold or bought

Love is eternal
In infinite supply
Love is within you
Love is the reason why

Love is intangible
It fills you up inside
Love yourself as you would another
And love's well will never run dry.

Love Thyself

Disrespected?
Made to feel small?
Be determined not
To tolerate this at all!

If someone can treat you
In such a way
They do not deserve
For you to stay

Respecting yourself
Is the key
To protecting yourself
From someone careless as he/she

Love yourself more
Than you love her/him
Then cut your losses
And you'll always win.

Lucid Dreams

I awakened once
But they sedated me again
So powerful was the drug they administered
My eye did close and fasten

Shut tight
Bolted down
How I've struggled to reopen
The portal I had found

Blinded by them
Plunged back into the dark
But I knew I'd seen the light
And they could not extinguish the spark

My faith was strong
They couldn't snuff it out
And there's always a chink, you see
Even in a black hole, no doubt

And though the door is heavy
And locked from the outside
Once you've been awake
The illumination does not subside

There's always a gentle glow
However dormant it seems
So draw the curtains if you wish
For I awaken and see in my dreams.

Luminaries

Luminaries
Celestial beings
Spiritual creatures
That come to see us

Heaven sent
To teach us things
Bring about rebirth
Inspire our imaginings

Starpeople
A phenomenon that's real
They rise to prominence
Provoke us to think and feel

Employing symbolism
Using subliminal signs
Enveloping them in music
To really blow our minds.

Make it STOP!!!

Branded have I been
Condemned to wear a badge of 'shame'
Repeatedly being stigmatised
By medical 'professionals' who like to blame

Every symptom I have
On the fact that TEN YEARS AGO
I happened to lose the plot
For a moment or so

Pinned at the top of my notes
Does it state this fact
And now it seems everything I experience
Must surely be traced back to that

I'm sick and tired of having to fight
To be taken seriously
I'm sick of having to pander and beg
So that never again will I not be free

It shouldn't be allowed
The slate should be wiped clean
I've done my time and toe the line
No relapses have there been

Well I refuse to take it anymore
Enough is now enough
And with the support of MIND
I will fight this – however tough

It is to get them to see
It's blatant discrimination
I deserve to be treated like anyone else
Regardless of the situation

So to anyone out there
Who's encountered the very same
And who is now battling
To clear their blackened name

Make that call
Get an advocate
And once and for all
Make the stigma STOP!

Marigolds Woes

You fill the bowl
To wash the pots
You make sure the water
Is scorching hot

Plenty of Fairy
To cut through the gunge
Then into the deep
Do your Marigolds plunge

But in a split second
You cry out in pain
A blood-curdling scream
There's a f**king hole in them again!

Your fingers are singed
You jump up and down
Wrestling with rubber
Dragging it down

Over your arms
As fast as you can
Revealing the blisters
All over your hands

How on earth
Did these Marigolds go
And foil me again
By acquiring a hole?

They're bloody brand-new
Only worn them once!
Yet somehow they're torn
And my digits are toast

Why does this happen?
Is there no God?
Invent some flaming rubber
Immune to the prod

Of a mystery hole punch
That wins every time
Incinerating my poor fingers
As I try to remove grime!

Surely there's an answer
An invention for that –
If only rubber gloves
Were made of shellac.

Mean Green

She put on a lilac 'rinse'
And left it for only ten mins
It went a deep shade of violet
She wished she hadn't tried it

So she attempted to wash it out
But it was stuck fast, there was no doubt
Then it faded to all colours of the spectrum
Now it's green and matches her plectrum

It wasn't her intention to have green hair
She wishes she'd resisted the urge
To dye it and make a right flaming mess
Now it seems in her head someone's purged

So every day she scrubs and scrubs
With all manner of paint strippers
But the green in her barnet just won't budge
So she's stuck with this colour it figures

Trying to match her clothes with her hair
Is proving quite a task
There's only so much teal in her closet
And she's bored with this situation, though it lasts

Sick of the sight
When she looks in the mirror
She feels like shaving it all off

Grotbags would be thrilled
That she had an impersonator
Oh, if only this girl could laugh!

But it's no laughing matter
When your hair's in tatters
And no amount of effort sorts it out

All she wants to do
Is vanquish this colour
But she can't and it's stressing her out!

Metamorphosis

Fallen from grace
What have I become?
An unfamiliar place
I stay though I should run

Unrecognisable
From the girl I was before
Utter loss of innocence
A worldlier aura takes the floor

I know when it began
Not so long ago
When fate dealt me a hand
And I couldn't take the blow

Since then I've just been floundering
Trying to climb up slippery walls
Reassembling the broken pieces
Into some semblance of what I was

I'll never be the same
The cracks may never heal
Though they're firm and held together
By something stronger than steel

Yes the 'vase' has been restored
But remains intrinsically changed
For once you've hit rock bottom
Some residue remains

It seeps into your very core
Polluting what was pure
And no amount of cleansing
Can purge so you're as before

You lose a piece of your soul
Something innate is torn
Thus ultimately a shadow appears
A scar where you weathered a storm

It changes you in the end
Where you were once carefree
Your aching heart does harden
Into rock where bleeding veins should be

Jaded though not bitter
A faint weariness in the subliminal
You wear a painted smile
Though underneath you succumb to cynical

And thus you act in accordance
With what you feel inside
And adopt associated behaviours
Attracting others who vibrate in kind

This new persona I've become
So different from the other one
Is yet another incarnation on this plane
Until I don my chrysalis once again.

Missed

Knew I missed you
But didn't realise how much
Until I saw your face
On a screen but couldn't touch

Until I saw your smile
The twinkle in your eye
That's when it hit me how much I miss you
That's when I wanted to cry

But I had to put on
A brave face, it's true
Couldn't let you see me breaking
Just couldn't do that to you

Because I know you'd do most anything
To be with me through difficult times
You even called your doctor
But he ordered you not to risk your life!

And so it is that we are miles apart
And I couldn't hug you on Mother's Day
The uncertainty and longevity
Of this lockdown just isn't OK

But if it means I'll have you for longer
I'll do whatever it takes
If it means you don't catch the virus
These sacrifices I will make

Just know that I've got my eye on you too
And am protecting you from a distance
And when the time's right I'll jump in my car
Even if I have to join the resistance

I love you, Mum,
More than words can describe
Look after yourself
Please stay inside.

Narked

I am myself
I belong to me
I don't belong to you
I shall set myself free

You have no power
Over me anymore
I no longer love you
For my heart is sore

From being drained of blood
When you wounded me so
That I could not heal
Or stem the flow

As I haemorrhaged
From being cut open wide
'Til my broken heart shrivelled
And almost died

'Til I could not breathe
From the searing pain
'Til I could not cry
Like clouds wrung out of rain

'Til I could not feel
For I'd turned to stone
A partial ice queen I became
For my blood ran cold

And thus did it die
The bond that we had
The bond that had made me
Always come back

Severed now forever
For you killed a part of me
No pulse have I
When it comes to thee

Ever the 'victim'
No remorse
No empathy
In denial, of course

Of what you really are –
A narcissist
Well, I've survived thus far
Now you are dismissed.

Not Quite Breakfast At Tiffany's…

Don't need my 'full English' served
On a giant rectangular slab
Don't need a dressed salad garnish
With my bacon, sausage and egg

Don't need vine-on cherry tomatoes
Give me canned ones in juice instead
And though I've scoured this ridiculous slab
Can I fook find a slice of fried bread?!

And where is my builder's tea?
English breakfast or Earl Grey's the choice
But cutlery won't stand up in either
I want Tetley's, nowt else will suffice

Oh, what has happened
To the greasy spoon?
This 'N8 Brunch'
Is loony tunes

Ten of my squid
For two brittle half rashers
That crumble to dust
When faced with my gnashers

One measly egg
Yet a goblet of beans
Presented as if made
Of priceless things

Resplendent on said slab
In a vessel all of their own
Yet still I detest these things
And deign to leave them alone

And every cuppa you have
Costs an additional fee
No bottomless beverages here
No meal deal where your tipple is free

This wasn't always the case
But gentrification is setting in
Prices soar, pretension is rife
Poshification of everything

I love London toon
Particularly Crouch End
But I'm northern at heart
And it drives me round the bend

When I'm being ripped off
Taken for a ride
Fleeced and shafted
Hung out and dried

If I pop down the road
To N22
A tenner will buy
Double the amount of food

Might not look as pretty
Might not be as 'posh'
But at least it's value for money
Not like detonating your dosh

Middey's by name
Midget by nature
The tiniest of fry-ups
Leaves me cold by temperature

A sprinkling of rocket
Is an utter abomination
On a British institution
I can't afford at this rate of inflation

So b***ocks to the balsamic
You sprinkled on those leaves
That didn't belong there in the first place
Desist in future, please!

Dispense with the vegetation
The slab that should be a plate
And reinstate the greasy spoon
In my beautiful N8.

Mirror, Mirror

When you look in the mirror
Do you like what you see?
Not talking appearances here
This isn't about vanity

I'm asking you can you look yourself in the eye?
Knowing what you have done?
Just because nobody found out
Doesn't mean that you have won

For you have to live with it every day
Your conscience ringing that bell
Incessantly 'til it just won't go away
Thus your life is a living hell

Is your reflection
Like the portrait of Gray?
Rotting and deteriorating from within?

Does it get uglier
With every passing day?
Each and every time you sin?

Depicting you as you really are
When examined from the inside out?
For that's where it counts and where lies the truth
Not in the lipstick you wear on your mouth

That mask you wear is a disguise
A painting that hides the cracks
A flimsy cover for secrets and lies
Until karma you in the face smacks

For heed these words
It all comes around
And one day there'll be nowhere to run

So make hay now
While the sun shines
Until justice to you is done.

Monotonous Mercury Rising

Unrelenting heat
Persists for protracted days
Outstaying its welcome now
Oppressive the lack of shade

Nowhere to escape and hide
From the blinding rays
Sweaty, sleepless nights
Wandering around in a daze

Fatiguing soaring temperatures
Sap vitality
Lounging is all I feel capable of
Low output, productivity

The air so densely humid
Almost another layer to bear
I yearn for the intermittent breeze
To cool and caress my hair

Gooey tarmac
Scorched white grass
Too prickly to sit
It scratches my asse

Too sweltering now to bask
And obtain a golden glow
Instead I dodge the searing fingers
That singe me as they stroke

From dawn 'til dark and into the night
The temperature persistently high
I toss and turn and beg for mercy
But it continues until it's light

Oh pretty please would you kindly
Turn it down a notch
It's boring now, really
To be so burning hot

Bring on the rain
To cleanse us all
Extinguish the furnace
Rehydrate, let it fall!

Drench my skin
Until I'm soaking wet
Bring about rebirth
I entreat, nay, I beg!

My Kryptonite

I see your face
My knees go weak
My kryptonite
I struggle to speak

How it excites me
When you are close by
I can't let you go
Not even gonna try

The scent of you
Really turns me on
Your delicious skin
When we are one on one

I think of you
When we are apart
No matter how far
Always in my heart

Through thick and thin
We still remain
I'll take the pleasure
And even the pain

Even your mood swings
Don't put me off
They're so James Dean
I have to laugh

Cool and sultry
With a little dash of fire
It makes me nervous
Though I pulse with desire

Your genius mind
Your silly jokes
You're my best friend
I love you so!

Narnia?

Have I been transported to Narnia?
The land of eternal snow?
Winter has fallen forever
Everything basks in its white glow

The lakes are frozen over
Thick ice has now set in
Encasing all of the water
Locking it safe within

Breathtaking is this sight
I struggle to compose myself
By day or by moonlight
This natural beauty my heart melts.

Noble Narcissus

Virginal and pure
She majestically stands
Rooted in the earth
Of this divine land

In her element
She radiates
Her delicate beauty
And contemplates

Her incarnation brief
Her only season spring
Until next year, of course
When she blossoms again

Youthful and fresh
Scented and sweet
Face towards the sun
Gazing up at me.

One Canada Square

The most iconic tower
In all of London town
Imposing and majestic
Gleaming in the sun

The windows a billion mirrors
Refracting rays of light
With a pyramid atop it
A flashing beacon of white

Symbolic of the city
Visible everywhere
Standing proud and pretty
Number One Canada Square.

One Love

'United we stand
Divided we fall'
Though we are physically separated
In this together are we all

So keep in touch
Communicate
Comfort each other
Do not spread hate

The future is uncertain
We know not what is to come
But we can still reach out
To each and everyone

This is the time
To cast aside
Our differences
And to each other be kind

We all are suffering
In different ways
We do not handle things
Exactly the same

Love each other
Now more than ever
If someone falls silent
Send them a message

Give someone a call
Suggest a video date
We know not when we'll meet again
So do not hesitate

We have the means
To stay connected
Virtually, verbally, vibrationally
Though bodily segregated

House Party, Skype
FaceTime and Zoom
Hours of fun
From your living room

There is no need
To feel alone
Even in self-isolation
There's always someone to phone

Any petty irritations
Perhaps one time you felt
Should now be instant history
For that person may perhaps need help

Open up your heart
As wide as you possibly can
Reveal your deepest feelings
Show abundant compassion

For in consciousness
We all are one
Intertwined
Daughters and sons

Soul to soul
Interlinked
Never island entities
Whatever you may think

When this eventually is over
Let us remember only that
What didn't kill us made us stronger
For each other was all we had.

People Police

Double standards
Hypocrisy
One rule for them
Another for thee

Tongues dripping with lies
The fangs are almost out
Better watch your back
Or you'll be pulling swords, no doubt

Under surveillance
The ever-watchful eye
Monitoring your every move
To see if you comply

Rules to be obeyed
Judgements in the ether
You have to respect their laws
Or expect a sermon from their preacher

Live and let live
Doesn't apply
You'll be reprimanded
Though you may not understand why

If they disagree with your actions
And the way you prioritise
Because it jars with them
And you eventually they despise

So be careful what you say
And how much you divulge
For it may be held against you
And all favour you had annulled

For familiarity
Breeds contempt
Sad but true
I lament

Best to put
Some space between
You and that 'force'
That notices everything

Take some distance
Step right back
Shield yourself
From unwarranted attacks

I guarantee
It's for the best
Extract yourself
From the vipers' nest.

Pink Roses

Baby-pink, sugary roses
Blossoming, in full bloom
Their delicious, floral fragrance
Envelopes my senses and I swoon

Bowled over by their sweetness
Their heavenly scent hangs in the air
So beautiful I want to pluck them
But I decide to leave them there.

PlusNOT!

Plusnet I hate you
Your customer service is dire
You just tell me lies
I want to set you on fire

I'm no arsonist
But it's been nearly a month
And still no flaming Wi-Fi
Now I've really got the hump

And I know all about humps
As I was recently on a camel
And through that I've learned to hiss and spit
And p**s like these unruly mammals

I've conquered sand dunes
On the back of these beasts
And shall take you down too
If you persist giving me beef

Should've been last week
Now it's going to be next
Stop moving the goal posts!
Can't you see how I'm vexed?!

You say there's a fault
On my line
That YOU disconnected
Then CHARGED me a fine!

You won't refund me
Until it's all been fixed
But fix it you can't
You complete and utter dicks!

I've spoken to OFFCOM
About my complaint
And drafted a letter
That clearly states

What berks you are
What incompetent buffoons!
To allow me to be slammed
Then rub salt into my wounds!

By making me pay
For the service I haven't got
It's laughable really
But I kid you not

So the saga continues:
I'm disconnected still
Hope you enjoyed the sequel
But to live I'm losing the will.

Preyed Upon

You've freaked me out
Feel violated
You tried to take advantage
Get me annihilated

You came prepared
With your 'Party Pack'
Your secret weapon
I was under attack

Unaware
Of what you had in mind
Naïve and green
And f**king blind

I couldn't see
'Cause I wasn't looking
Your hidden agenda
Disguised as a good thing

The oldest trick
In the book
In spite of #metoo
You tried your luck

I trusted you
Thought you were a pro
But you're a waste of space
So p**s off and go

Crawl back under
Your slimy rock
Got no time for vile predators
Who are ruled by their c**ks.

Projectile Bile

The uncaring and un-empathic
Make me oh so mad
Thoughtlessly operating
They carelessly fire around

Insensitive words
That can prick and sting
Designed to hurt
Dark energy do they bring

It's all about them
And their world of pain
So bitter and twisted
Verbal punches do they rain

Down on those
Whom have 'irked' them so
Unwittingly perhaps
But still they blow

Me, me, me!
They take precedence
Self-centred to the hilt
So others they condemn

Offloading at the innocent
To numb their misery inside
Makes them feel better
To cause another to cry

I guess they can't help it
As they're suffering within
Something is lacking
In them, something grim

So on to any poor soul
Do they their bile project
Thus be mindful of this
And yourself do protect.

Psst...!

Indiscretion
Is an unfortunate trait
Igniting rumours
Spreading hate

Lighting fires
Where waters were calm
With the intention of causing
Somebody harm

Sullying a reputation
Dropping poison in willing ears
The Ten Of Swords is dealt
Backstabbing the tactic of fear

The cowardly assailant
Dishing dirt from behind the scenes
A malevolent Wizard Of Oz
Manipulating things

And minions with loaded guns
Patrol now they've been 'armed'
Programmed, remotely controlled
By the Wizard which has them charmed

Poised to attack
When the 'enemy' draws near
Enlisted to fight someone else's war
Not to support any cause they hold dear

Embroiled in something
That concerns them not
Having leapt on the bandwagon
Intent on thickening the plot

Oh, the Wizard had swallowed a bitter pill
Which caused it to vent its spleen
With bias and embellishment
It'd carefully set the scene

Cast itself as the innocent victim
In a fairy tale
It'd relayed to its little minions
Itself the hero that must prevail

They writhed and they seethed
Utterly taken in
By the Wizard's fantastical story
Believing everything

And their blood began to boil
Then it bubbled and it blistered
And its putrid bile did overflow
Into a sea of Chinese Whispers.

Pumpy Pumpkins

Pumpkins, pumpkins
Orange, plump and juicy
Spicy in a pie
Or hollowed out and spooky

Perfect in a curry
To warm your winter heart
But be sure not to overdose
Or they may just make you fart!

Question

What does it all mean?
This life we lead
We rise with the sun
We love, we bleed

On a treadmill
Moving day to day
We go through the motions
And act a certain way

We while away the hours
At work and at leisure
We indulge in a few
Gratifying earthly pleasures

And the clock ticks on
No respite in sight
What's it all for?
Why does day turn into night?

A cyclical existence
The huge wheel turns
Some say it's a challenge
We're here to learn

We're born, we die
The interim's a choice
But fate has a hand
In whether we commiserate or rejoice

I know not what
I incarnated for
But the monotony is palpable
And I crave something more.

Rabid and Racist

You never really know someone
What goes on in their minds
Until the apple cart is overturned
And they let rip with words unkind

Until they feel slighted
Which in fact they got so wrong
And they accuse you of despicable deeds
That their paranoid mind has spun

And so it transpires you're a 'liar'
Then evidence they demand
Apparently you're on trial
They're the judge and jury, they command

You to produce something
That actually doesn't exist
You tell them so
But they won't let it go
And so they persist and persist

And then they start
To hurl RACIAL abuse
At your 'Englishness'
And the cannon comes loose

It hits the deck
Explodes in a fury
The red mist arises
You attack in a frenzy

Unleashing a verbal
Firing squad
On the defence
Against a slanderous sod

So far removed
From reality
Utterly deranged
And too blind to see

You actually told the truth
And never did lie
They just chose not to believe
Although you did try

So another 'friendship'
Bites the dust
To come to such a cropper
It clearly wasn't robust

But to be racially slurred
Your character assassinated
Shows such a low opinion
Of you – you're exasperated

And such a contempt for the natives
Of the country they occupy
When they blatantly state
They'd rather not integrate
With the 'English' they clearly despise

So beware who you trust
For a viper can lurk
'Neath the costume of an ally
Ready to bite you and go berserk

Their true colours surfacing
And the venom they've concealed
Rising to the surface
With a turn of the wheel.

Rebirth

As the wheel turned
A new cycle began
She shed the last like a skin

She prayed that a butterfly
Would materialise
From the ugly cocoon she'd been in

Shackled, in chains
For way too long
Finally she'd broken free

Opened her eyes
As if for the first time
Like she'd been blind but now could see

A shift in perspective
As she regarded her face
Reflected back from the glass

No longer macabre
But cleansed and fresh
Forgiven and purged at last

The self-loathing that afflicted
Had burnt itself out
All had been forgiven

Now she was at peace
Within and without
Thanks to reciting the act of contrition

And thus a clean slate
A blank page was laid out
Full of potential and promise

All she need do
Was write the next chapter
And venture forward as honest

As she possibly could be
With herself and the world
No hiding behind smokescreens

For only by being
True to yourself
Can you live the life of your dreams.

Red Alert!

Panic stations all around
Out of bed like it's on fire
Going to Marrakesh in nine days
And my passport has expired!

Working full time
Easter in between
Only one working day
To go and see the queen

Tried to sort it all online
Computer says bloody 'no'
Battling to wake up sans caffeine
But to the post office I must go

Thanking f**k
It's actually open
Now it's been privatised

In this case
Flogging it off
Is actually saving lives

Grabbed a form in a frenzy
Blurted out my dilemma
Fortunately the guy on the counter
Helped me keep my s**t together

"Panic not, the form's really easy
"Renewal the simplest option
"Now get yourself to Snappy Snaps
For some mugshots for identification."

Well, I look so rough I want to cry
But time is of the essence
Not enough for slap and a blow-dry
When there's no time like the present

So off I pop with under-eye bags
And creases on my face from sleep
I look so rotten I terrify children
As I hurry down the street

She takes my pics in a flash (lol)
This camera sure as hell better lie
The wrinkles I've acquired since the last
Are so savage I want to die

With limp bed hair
And puffy cheeks
I may need a counter-signatory

The girl in the original
Passport shot
Undetectable in the older horror story

I pay the bill all the same
And shuffle off out of the shop
I blame the photographer for causing me pain
Not the fact my hair's like a mop

Not the fact I've aged
Well, it has been ten flipping years!
Guess I should consider Botox
And wipe away my tears

Anyway I'm lucky
For I live in the smoke
And Her Maj has a free appointment
On the one day I can actually go!

So I've completed the form
As careful as can be
Stumped up the dosh
So the country I can flee

Thus this catastrophe
Has a seemingly happy ending
And I can face my mum
Without having lost all the money we're spending

On a mini trip of a lifetime
For how flaming would she be?
If we'd paid but couldn't go in the end?
Because of a ditsy dumb-ass like me?!

Red Flag

She is lunar
She waxes and she wanes
Her cycle like the moon
Mystical power she contains

Her moods like the tide
Changing day by day
Hormonally riding
The crests of these waves

Encounter her at the beginning
And enticing is she
Beguiling to be around
Inside her he wants to be

Yet lo, when the heat has cooled
She wants to be alone
Her claws may come out
If he should get too close

Inward she turns
To examine how she feels
Deep into her psyche goes she
And neon are her dreams

Then comes the flow
A clearing oft with pain
She needs to be nurtured
Sheltered from the crimson rain

So shower her with love
Or leave her, blessed be
Now is the time to retreat
Replenish her energy

Whatever you do, don't wave
A red flag in her face
She may not be a bull
But this cow can rage and chase

Beware the wild woman
Disturbed from her meditative state
Goad her at your peril now
Avoid encountering the grimmest fate

For this dazzling goddess can turn
In the blinking of an eye
Akin to the preying mantis
Devouring her guy

'Til nothing else remains
Save for the memory
Of their encounter in her mind alone
For exist no more would he.

Red Mist

Tomorrow is
A brand-new day
Hopefully by then
All this fury will have gone away

I may not sleep
For I seethe through every pore
My blood is boiling
I rage like a wild boar

But I will bite my tongue
For now at least
And to my addled mind
I shall endeavour to restore peace

I gave you the benefit
Of the doubt
But your retort fuelled the flames
And the furnace is yet to burn out

I fear I saw your true colours
And did they I despise
A wolf in sheep's clothing
Diminished could you be in my eyes

I may have misconstrued
The words that you wrote
Yet I suspect I did not
For on language do you also dote

Thus lying livid
In my bed
Your careless words
Resound in my head

The wound you inflicted
Gaping and sore
Compounded by the distinct lack
Of a shred of remorse

I want to curse you
Proclaim you a c**t
Expletives seem the only
Appropriate response

But I know how unpretty
Unbridled anger can be
The one human emotion
We should sugarcoat, apparently

Shouldn't we all just project
Sweetness and holy light?
Hoy realism out the window
Pretend everything's all right?

Vomit stunning sunbeams?
S**t huge rainbows and stars?
Not disclose the ugly stuff
Conceal our permanent scars?

Yes, I digress
But despite what I've gleaned
I feel certain things
Are better out than in

Otherwise they brew
Toxify your insides
Drive you insane
Or cause you to commit crimes

I never killed anyone today
I simply vented my spleen
Using prose
As opposed to a machine

Gun trained on the object
Of my wrath
Though the red mist did rise
There was no actual bloodbath.

Red Sky

A Sahara/strawberry sky
Hangs over London Town
Shrouded in a sultry fog
As from my tower I peer out

The view across the city
Takes on a *Blade Runner*esque hue
As fiction threatens to come to life
With Ophelia passing through

The mood reactively ominous
The calm before the storm
Nobody wishes anyone
To come to any harm

The streetlights all aglow
Though it's only 4pm
Eerily silent and unseasonably warm
Are we facing Armageddon?

Red layers of ancient sand
Sail in on the balmy wind
From the deserts of Africa
Of biblical times do they remind

Thus this hurricane adopts a fleece
So innocuous does she seem
As did her namesake when in death
And floating down the stream

But like the flowers she loved so
This beauty we cannot trust
For it has the power to maim and kill
When its eye is at last upon us.

Ring Burn

When I wedged it on
Never knew it'd get stuck fast
Was trying to be stylish
Not induce a life-or-death dash

To the emergency room
When the soap and Fairy liquid failed
And my poor damn finger turned purple
Swelled up and caused me to wail

I had to dial 111
They told me there was no hope
Unless I went to A&E
To get it sawn off – I swear, no joke!

Thus off I went
In the dead of night
It was pouring down
But I needed out of this plight

With a throbbing, fat finger
I arrived at The Whitt
Registered at reception
Was undoubtedly deemed a twit

Sat in the waiting room
For what seemed an eternity
But this penance had to be endured
If my finger was to be freed

From its nickel shackle
That squeezed and nipped and pinched
From the allergic reaction
That caused it to blister and itch

When they finally called my name
And I sheepishly met the nurse
She almost fell about laughing
At this mishap that evoked her mirth

But she ushered me through
Quickly anyway
To an operating theatre
Where to my dismay

I clocked an array of tools
That scared the life out of me
Metal cutters, chainsaws and knives
Sharpened beyond belief!

Wielding them
She grabbed my hand
Clamped the offending
Fake gold band

Yanked and sliced
Wrenched and stretched
Prised that b*stard
As I screamed and wept

Until the foreign body
Was completely off
And my finger could breathe
Unencumbered by that sod

Oh how it f**king hurt!
How it singed and it burned!
It felt like being dismembered
But thankfully my digit remained

Oh, hallelujah!
Did I then sing
They had succeeded
In removing the ring!

Unbelievably
They'd saved my life
And rescued me
From this particular strife.

Rioja

Velvety smooth
Fruity, full and rich
It cascades down my throat
Having passed my lips

Slowly but surely
Its warmth permeates
I feel myself unwind
Savouring the taste

Cheeks all aglow
As I settle down
The perfect way
To soothe a furrowed brow

Its colour deep and regal
It insulates on chilly nights
Snuggled up in bed
With a glass by my side

Sipping it so carefully
Savouring every drop
The divine taste of Rioja
Is something that I love.

Sandy Saharan Story

The sun sets over the Sahara
A blinding fireball in the sky
The dunes ablaze with golden light
As day unveils the night

The crimson sand cooling
Its ember coals fade to grey
The searing heat subsides
A light breeze caresses our face

The Bedouin campsite beckons
Like nomads we wend our way
Sandblasted skin and eyes aglow
The candlelit marquee awaits

Warmly greeted by the desert tribe
We are served mint tea and almonds
Opulence abounds as we take respite
Tucked away in the Saharan mountains

Illuminated harlequin lanterns
Embedded in the ground
Depict our passage through
The rouge-carpeted sandy mounds

A feast of bricochette poulet
And legumes graces the table
We dine and share our experiences
And hear tales and Arabic fables

And then the entertainment begins
As we gather around the bonfire
Beating drums and acoustic strings
Symphonise our every melodic desire

Into late evening
We chant and we sing
A melting pot of nationalities
United in hymn

The noir velvet darkness
Studded with an abundance of electric stars
Twinkling at the tips of our noses
A sparkling canopy igniting our hearts

At the stroke of midnight
We eventually bed down
The final curtain drawn
The jewel in the crown

The sheer majesty of the Sahara
Is breathtaking beyond words
Her soothing ambience and tranquility
A mystical wonder of this earth.

Sayonara

Frenemy, frenemy there you are
Your true colours finally shown
An ugly palate of murky shades
I'd suspected but not fully known

Your guard let down
They came to light
In an outpouring of harboured rage

That clearly had
Been festering inside
Until this putrid and vile display

Like a rocket gone off
And a woman possessed
You listed all of my 'sins'

Instructed me
To live vacuously
Or be cast out with the bins

I chose the latter
For not for me
Are 'friends' of the fair-weather kind

A friend should be someone
Who's got your back
You can laugh with and unwind

But more than that
They must show respect
Even when times get tough

Never must
That line be crossed
Or the whole thing will combust

And combust it did
In spectacular style
Past the point of no return

As one by one
Insult by insult
Every bridge did you burn

Thus cut loose are you
And banished for life
No regrets and no great loss

In separating
The wheat from the chaff
New horizons can I cross

Out with the old
And in with the new
As the energy starts to shift

Already they come
The influx begins
Of new friends bearing their gifts

So sayonara
And good luck too
As we walk our separate paths

I shed you now
For pastures new
Never to look back.

Secret Garden

Secret garden
In full bloom
The hidden world
Of a mystical womb

Inside the well
A chalice lies
The Holy Grail
From Jesus' time

Hallowed ground
On the ley lines
A sacred place
For pilgrims to unwind

Magical landscape
Infused with heaven's scent
Which Merlin safeguards
With quiet intent.

Sharks

Swimming in perilous waters
Playing the dating game
Too many sharks for this little fish
Don't want to get bitten again

First they swoop
All over you like a rash
Making plans
Moving too fast

They build up your hopes
Infiltrate your dreams
Then they drop you
Just as quickly it seems

Having led you on
But having still played the field
They've cast their nets wide
But penetrated your shield

You let your guard down
Just for a while
They reeled you in
Then cast you aside

Left you hanging
Up in the air
Then next time you checked
They were no longer there

Blue-ticked and ghosted
Whilst they're clearly online
Chatting to another catch, no doubt
As you fall to the back of the line

Well competing's not for me
If I don't stand out from the crowd
You're clearly not of me worthy
So that's it, I'm done, I'm out.

Shelling Out

Shellac looks real pretty
It's also tough and gritty
But when it's chipped and shitty
You have to again dive into your kitty
Which is a pity

You can't just whip it off
For that varnish is bloody tough
It's made of very strong stuff
And a chisel ain't enough
Which is rough

It requires professional help
Heavy duty acid to make it melt
Then they scrape it off, which is hell
Every chunk when it's peeled can be felt
Which makes you yelp

So you pay them to put it on
And you wear it a while which is fun
But when you're finally done
You must pay again to make it gone
Which is a con

So enough of shellac have I had
For the expense is driving me mad
Never again will I succumb to this fad
Unless a lottery win do I have
Which is sad

It's a waste of tinfoil after all
To have your mitts so adorned
You could almost plug them into a wall
And power the entire street from dusk 'til dawn
Which could cause a fireball

Then you'd be totally fried
And have no need for shellac, which once tried
Is so addictive it bleeds your bank dry
Until you wake up and see the light
Which is right

Traditional nail polish is best
Though the fumes do play hell with your chest
And it don't last as long as the rest
But at least it's not much to invest
Which is the test

So I'm sodding the shellac
Giving gels the sack
To basics I'm going back
Using the old laq
Which is cheaper, albeit crap
And that is that.

Skin Deep

Ironically when at hospital
I went to get weighed
When I bent to remove my shoe
My Lycra leggings frayed

Nay, they royally ripped
Below my left butt cheek
A gaping hole appeared
White knickers for all to see

A pound of flesh
And half of my bum
On display
With nowhere to run

I'd like to think
They shrank in the wash
Clean on today
But that's probably tosh

For when I hit the scales
The needle went up
To sixty-four kilos
I couldn't bare to look

Middle-aged spread
Is afflicting me
Five foot three and a half
Curves for all to see

I can recall when
I was a mere seven stone
Twenty-one years old
Slender, lithe and toned

No problem squeezing
Into purple spandex jeans
Like Sandy's in *Grease*
Shiny black, final scenes

Back when I was
A perfect size six
Blonde and willowy
Before the clock ticked

To February 2020
My forty-fifth year
So much has changed
Not just the size of my rear

Maturing disgracefully
Although that's about to change
For although my foot is fractured
I'm no longer in so much pain

Instead I'm focusing inward
Repairing my wounded soul
Reinventing the 'wheel'
Recovery my goal

And there's so much work
Still to be done
I haven't time to fret
Over the size of my bum

That's one good thing about ageing
You sure as hell care less
About outward appearances
And your hair being a mess

For it's what's inside that counts
And if you're discontented
You'll never be satisfied
And lost youth may be lamented

Don't fear growing old
And developing some padding
It's better than the alternative
Or being emaciated and sagging

Embrace your waist
The extra inch or two
Love yourself
Then you won't have to

Obsess about your looks
And any lines that appear
You won't need to seek approval
Or the coming decades fear

And if you're inclined
To seek solace in prayer
That sense of connection
Will form a protective layer

Around your insecurities
And put them to bed
Amplify your inner voice
So you can hear that instead

Of any self-defeating thoughts
About your evolving looks
Until you actually no longer do
Give a flying f**k

You'll no longer need a mask
For beauty comes from within
You'll find inner peace at last
And feel comfortable in your own skin.

Slacks

My 'tights' are falling down
I'm indecently exposed
My bum keeps hanging out
Of my baggy pantyhose

Every time I walk
They slither down my legs
And try as I might to discreetly hoist them up
They plummet to the ground instead

My 'tights' are falling down
If before I'd left home I'd known
I'd have doubled up on knickers
To ensure they didn't drop down

Should've shopped in M&S
And maybe they would've stayed up
Should've hired a crane
Or worn suspenders but no such luck

My 'tights' are falling down
But right now there's nothing I can do
So if you should see my bum
I sincerely apologise to you.

It's not because they're old
Or because the elastic has snapped
It's because I bought them in Primark
And frankly they are crap

My 'tights' are falling down
Like I said before
They should really be renamed 'slacks'
Because they're virtually on the floor.

Slave To Fashion

Clearing out the clutter
Is definitely no mean feat
When your cupboards are exploding with crap
Because you're a hoarder like me

I like to collect clothes
I've had some since 1999
Half of which don't fit
Though I'll never give up trying

Apparently three wardrobes
And a man-size cupboard
Two whopping chests of drawers
Aren't enough space so I'm buggered

Therefore got to bite the bullet
And shed a load of gear
The charity shop will love me
Though I'll be also shedding some tears

When you're like me
Nothing goes out of fashion
And flamboyant dressing
Is one of my passions

The actress in me
Likes to get titivated up
Thus I've a range of costumes
All manner of get-ups

Sometimes I look a sight
But I really have such fun
Assembling my outfits
Come snow, sleet, rain or sun

The Imelda Marcos
Of Crouch End
A million pairs of shoes
And of coats, about ten thousand

A vast selection of frocks
In an array of sizes
Woolly jumpers galore
And let's not forget the trousers

Then there's the skirts
And a plethora of tops
And last but not least
Pyjamas, gym wear and the knickerbox

So many garments
For so many occasions
I need a walk-in closet
That I lack one is a source of frustration

I've even used up the space
Underneath my bed
It's chock-a-block with scarves and hats
Because the wardrobe is on its last legs

The door fell off today
For honestly it's full to the brim
And in trying to force it shut
I've gone and destroyed the hinge

A lesson at last to be learned
Time to admit I suppose
That I'm a shopaholic
And hopelessly addicted to clothes

I blame that bloody snake
In the Garden Of Eden
For if Adam and Eve hadn't scoffed the forbidden fruit
We'd be butt-naked whatever the season

But the swine, he made them sin
And to cover their abject shame
They attired themselves with fig leaves
Never to be starkers again

And fig leaves led to fashion
They say *The Devil Wears Prada*
And that snake was the devil in question
Thus possessed am I by that blighter

An exorcism perhaps
Would be more suited to my needs
Or perhaps nudity could hit the catwalks
And become trendy then I would be freed!

Dream on, you silly bint!
For, alas, that clearly won't happen
So continue to purge or resist the urge
To be a dedicated slave to fashion.

Smashed

Crash, bang, wallop
She collided with the shelf
A free-standing unit
Until she grabbed it to steady herself

Down did it topple
Raining glass on her head
Sending everything flying
Through the air, what a mess!

Wine glasses, flutes, tumblers
And a vase
All hit the deck
And smashed into shards

Oh, what a racket
And a mess to behold
The nincompoop just stood there
And couldn't be consoled

But it's no use crying
Over veritable spilt milk
And in her inebriated state
The thought of cleaning did she jilt

Drunk and disorderly
She sent herself to bed
Knowing that tomorrow
She'd have a thumping head

So leaving shattered glass
All over the floor
Off did she teeter
To think about it no more

In the afternoon
When at last she awoke
The carpet was glistening
As if covered in snow

It shone and it sparkled
Like a night of a thousand stars
She wondered what'd occurred
Until her memory was jarred

By treading barefoot
Onto a sizeable piece of glass
That tore into her instep
Causing her to curse

Jumping up and down
With stinging, bleeding feet
She surveyed the considerable damage
Shocked at the scene

Of all her lovely glassware
Lying broken on the floor
A shattered picture frame
A teacup that was no more

Oops, thought she
What a flaming disaster
I'd better get a shovel
And hoover up straight after

And so she did
And all was fine
Apart from the gash
Which would heal in time

The moral of this story
Is nail your shelves down
And don't put glass atop them
If you're a drunken clown.

Snake In The Grass

Would you jump
Into my grave as quick?
If I was dead
Would you want a bit?

A piece of the action
Would you cling on to my coat tails
And be a stowaway in my coffin
Or basically into my back fire nails?

Just like with the Ten Of Swords
I am almost dead
Will you now hijack the angel
I fly to heaven with?

Without having the courtesy
To simply ask for a lift
Would you rather be a snake in the grass
Sneak around and hiss?

You're not the first
And I doubt you'll be the last
I've seen the likes of you before,
Mr Snake In The Grass

And no matter how many times
I've heard this expression before
Imitation ain't the highest form of flattery
It's a parasite feasting on you from behind closed doors

All you had to do
Was be upfront and honest
Tell me what you were up to
Instead of keeping it under the bonnet

Well, you've violated my trust
And it will never be restored
Safe to say I don't need
A 'friendship' like yours

To ensure I learn from this
I'll consign you to the scrap heap
Cut all ties hence forth
For I can do without deceit

And in future evermore
Will I my own counsel keep
For why should you off the back of
another's hard work
Such precious benefits reap?!

Snow Joke!

And so the snow finally came
But it didn't prevent me from getting to work
'Twas a bloody signal failure
That drove me bloody berserk

Battled through the ice
Skated the pavements and rode a bus
Travelled on the tube
Finally reached Highbury & Is

To find all Stratford trains cancelled
Though I waited and waited – in vain
To discover said signal failure
Had afflicted TFL again

Oh what a merry cock-up!
I feared the weather would be the culprit
That ultimately prevented me reaching
My destination – but that wasn't it

When will these signals be fixed?
Is a snowflake their kryptonite?
They're always breaking down
And must be considerably sh*te

To render a whole line defunct
A station unreachable
To cause them to send everyone home
And make them miserable

So back the way I came I trudged
Developing frostbite, hypothermic and miffed
All the while sending explanatory emails
To my bosses who could've been p****d

That on the very day of my appraisal
The most important one of the year
I couldn't make it to the office
Due not to snow but signal failure

The same old boring chestnut
That repeatedly blights the lives
Of poor, downtrodden commuters
Who are robbed by the extortionate price

Of a beyond sub-standard service
They are forced everyday to endure
They have no choice, it's a sacrifice
They undoubtedly wish they could be spared

Well, thank heavens I had my laptop
Having feared I'd be snowed in
But like I said 'twas bloody signal failure
That foiled me once again.

SOS

Weighed down by the heavy cloak of depression
And his tormented brain
He searched for the answers in a bottle
He reached the bottom and sank even deeper into the pit

Senses intoxicated
Clearly not in his right mind
He fumbled around in the medicine cabinet
Seeking the ultimate way out

The pills were calling out to him
"We can free you"
So he swallowed the lot
Washed down by liquor

The chemicals began to dance through his veins
Releasing their deadly poison
He was overcome
Unconsciousness set in
Contorted and convulsing he buckled and slumped to the floor

She found him this time
Like the time before
Out cold, black mucus running out of his mouth
His 'guardian angel'
She dialled 999

Twenty years later
And history repeats itself
This time he phones her to confess
The cycle resumes
Frantic calls to the authorities
Interminable waiting
Can he be brought back from the brink?

Yet again he is saved
But not cured
A ticking bomb free to wreak havoc
Upon his blood ties
Unharnessed rage and anger
Eluding the 'system' once more

A life saved
But a life sentence imposed on his 'loved' ones
When will it ever end?!

"Soft, Strong, Here's Hoping The Sheeple Ain't Wrong"

Television stations
Need to get with the programme
Now that we're rationing
And heading for lockdown

Pardon the pun
But they're so passé
The cheffy shows
Are completely out of date

Ready Steady Cook
Come Dine With Me
Using ingredients
That I haven't seen

For nearly a week
In any of the shops
But I'm salivating and yearning
As I helplessly watch

For all I've got to play with
Is a packet of cream crackers
A strip of barbecue spare ribs
And some sun-dried tomatoes

A few digestives
And soft Brussels sprouts
Instant noodles
Until I can next leave the house

And Lord knows when that'll be
For my throat's a little sore
And I'm about to paint
A red plague cross on my door

I'm quarantined
For the foreseeable
Fast running out of soap
Without any paracetamol

Been trying to stock up
But it's impossible round here
Thus this is what happens
When people give in to fear

So I'm having to make do
With what I've actually got
And fortunately for me
Bog roll WAS in stock!!!

So I can wipe my a*se
Until the cows come home
Which means I'll survive corona!
As we all KNOW that's the antidote!

The Holy Grail!
The magic pill!
So who gives a fook?
If I'm getting physically ill?!

I'm invincible!
With Andrex by my side!
Though I'm bracing myself somewhat
For this roller coaster ride.

Stalemate

Left in limbo
Suspended in mid-air
Swinging neither left nor right
The Hanged Man can but stare

Can't make any plans
Or even act upon
My intense gut instinct
That currently burns so strong

The wheel is a-turning
Certain things must fall away
But the motion is too slow
And I'm stuck 'til it shifts again

Patience never was
A virtue of mine
Impulsive I am
Once I've made up my mind

I long to break free
From the shackles I am in
But circumstance dictates
I must pause for the interim

Everything hinges
On what happens next
I await my opponent's move
In this interminable game of chess

It seems we're in check
But I pray not in mate
I may be a pawn
But it's still not too late

The underdog can triumph
In spite of the odds
It's not always the case
That prevails the law of sods

The universe must provide
If one plays by the rules
Adheres to its principles
Then no way can one lose

So I'll bide my time
Meditate and pray
That the solution for my highest good
Ultimately comes my way.

Steaming Hardcore

Unbelievably I was just offered
An actual VAGINAL STEAMING
My WTF?! expression
Shows I've no concept of its meaning

But I sure as hell don't intend
To suspend my little miff
Over a pan of boiling water
If you get my drift?!

I've never been good at squatting
Even whilst in Japan
Those Asian loos defeated me
I fell straight into the can

So don't even think about
Asking me to hover
Over a contraption
That will get me hot and bothered

Right where the sun don't shine
In a ritualistic fashion
Surrounded by a ring of hippies
Who'll be watching me and chanting

Whilst I apparently perch
On a floral-bedecked commode
Filled with liquid and herbs
With my legs akimbo

My foo-foo now on fire
As it naturally begins to cook
'Til I can't sit down for a month
Without screaming as loud as fook!

Who the hell invented
This ridiculous New Age game?
It gives another dimension
To the entire vaping craze

How addicted must one be
To nasty nicotine?
If one's mouth and also one's
minge
Needs a hit or three?

VAGINAL STEAMING?
Are you out of your mind?!
My labia aren't legumes
To be served with butter and thyme

If your 'yoni' is that filthy
That soap and water won't do
And it needs industrial cleaning
Combined with magic too

To make it pristine again
At least spare us the spectacle
Of doing it in public
It's just not acceptable

To contaminate my newsfeed
With such a load of trash
Expecting me to cough up
For an assault like this on my gash

I'd probably never recover from
And certainly never live down
What exactly do you take me for?
You 'right on', crazy clown!

Normally I love
A bit of alternative s**t
I sometimes talk to unicorns
But this just takes the p**s

So thank you but no thanks
Though I'm all for Flower Power
I'll maintain the hygiene of my flaps
When I am in the shower.

Suds Law

Oh, what a bloody palaver
At Crouch End Boots today
When a jobsworth got in a lather
And actually turned me away

For daring to try to buy
What she deemed contraband
Refusing to let me purchase
My all-time favourite brand

Of L'Oreal Elvive
Colour Protect Shampoo
Because she told me it was NON-ESSENTIAL
Even though I'd queued

For almost HALF AN HOUR
After trying Superdrug first
But it was out of stock there
So to Boots did I revert

Since when was washing your hair
A flaming luxury?
Isn't a scrub with shampoo?
Vital to keep it clean?

I'll be utterly damned
If I'm going to be seen
With a barnet full of lard –
It's basic human hygiene!

I don't want to invite
A swarm of nasty fleas
To take up residence upon my head
Because it's swimming in grease

And I'm pretty sure a virus
Could also potentially lurk
Amongst any filthy curls
You prize, Gestapo-esque berk!

I walked away in disgust
But I was boiling with rage
To have had my time wasted so
And to be sans mop-cleaner was insane

I decided to call the store
And speak to the manageress
Who totally got my plight
And understood my intense distress

She told me it was absurd
That her assistant was talking bollocks
She invited me to go back
A red rag to this shopaholic!

So vindicated off I trotted
To claim what was rightfully mine
Eager to once again have
Hair that gleamed and shined

The Gestapo was still on the door
And clearly under duress
She was lamenting to a customer
That she was experiencing rudeness

Well, I thought, that's karma
What goes around does come around
What you give out do you get back
Engage your brain before you open your mouth!

I got my goods in the end
Though I was accused of pushing in
And ranted at by a lone old lady
But I took it on the chin

The important thing was that
I'd made a valid point
Consistency and common sense
Was lacking at this joint

Shampoo IS an essential item
And shouldn't require a permit
We've a right to wash our hair
Because we're bloody worth it.

Sunset Of My Life

Epic sunset
Emblazoned sky
Emotionally evocative
Its beauty makes me cry

Atop the snow-capped mountains
Illuminating the fjords
An explosion of magnificent colour
Forever to be adored

Unforgettable
Moving beyond belief
Tattooed on my mind for eternity
To visit when seeking peace.

Sweet Dreams

And so to bed
My weary body goes
Heavy and aching
I lift my toes

Onto the mattress
And lie comfortably down
Pulling close the duvet
I cocoon myself in its mound

Drowsiness takes over
I settle my head
Into the pillow
Close my eyes and rest

It's been a long day
And I'm feeling weak
Goodnight world
I'm off to sleep.

Swinging In The Meadow

The child on the swing
Deep in thought
Began to sing
And called out to God

"Embrace me," said she,
"I'm feeling lost,
"Take me in your arms,
"Let me feel your touch."

Rocking was she
Suspended in her cradle
Losing track of time
Her heart laid out on the table

And then a robin appeared
Landed right by her side
He turned to her, red breast aflame
In the glorious morning sunlight

He hopped around her
Never averting his gaze
He cocked his little head
And then flew off to another place

The child on the swing felt soothed
'Twas almost Christmas after all
Thus the sugary frost on the grass
And the robin who'd answered her call

Suggested that all would be well
If she trusted and just checked in
She held the key to the sacred chamber
Where they waited for her to begin

To commune with them
Her soul family
Who would listen without dismay

To all her woes and happy tales
And who then
Words of wisdom would say

They never left her
'Twas she who didn't visit
Thus she floundered there for a while

The lines were down
She was disconnected
And frankly the feeling was vile

Like a boat cast out on the ocean
With its compass spinning around
Battered by the waves and the wind
The tide almost ran her aground

But at last she'd found her anchor
And lowered it quickly to stop
Her vessel making her dizzy
Set adrift and running amok.

Taxing Taxes

Tax doesn't have to be taxing
When you're organised
But if you're like me and disorderly
You might find your brain gets fried

When you're drowning in receipts
When you're statements aren't there
And you're losing sleep
So you're tearing out your hair

When the dates are a mess
And you need to do your best
To file them chronologically
But you don't think logically

When you wear a million hats
How do you claim for that?
Along with the day job
You're a Jack Of All Trades – oh God!

The poor mind boggles
And the floor can't be seen
It's buried under paperwork
The poor bloody trees!

If I was paperless
Would I be less stressed?
Should I fork out for Quick Books?
Would then I more give a f**k?

About maintaining my accounts?
All year round?
If I did them monthly
Would I be less grumpy?

Then I ventured to the post office
In need of a break
The deadline is looming
Only a fine at stake!

I wondered if I bought
Some kind of box
To store my receipts
I'd feel less lost?

A special tin
To put them in
All neat and tidy
But I was undecided

Then I found a folder
With loads of pockets
A concertina thing
And it really rocked it!

All colours of the rainbow
Were the slots
With monthly little labels
And it didn't cost a lot

Besides not to worry
About the price
I can expense that
Which is ever so nice!

So I bought the thing
Then an old lady cried,
"Oooh, where was that?"
And I pointed to the side

Of the stand
Next to the till
"It's got loads of pockets,
"I think it's brill,

"I'm doing my taxes
"Always last minute!"
The old lady laughed:
"I know! Me too! Innit!"

And so we had a chuckle
A happy interlude
To break the monotony
Of the Tax Return Blues.

TFL Hell

The rush hour commute across London
By bus, Tube or train
Like sardines in a can
Or rats up a drain

Herded like cattle
Ranted at by TFL
Hamsters on a wheel
A daily taste of hell

Personal space invaded
Rammed against each other in a cage
No wonder some people lose it
Consumed with frustration and rage

Exposed to each other's odour
We sweat and we perspire
Germs gleefully multiply
A breeding ground, they spread like fire

Mingling with
'The great unwashed'
A mosh pit of misery
How do they justify the cost?!

Delays, cancellations,
Overcrowded stations close
Locked on the street
Crowds gather, nowhere to go

If you can get into the station
The platform's five lines deep
With people clamouring to board
A bottleneck of bewildered sheep

What the solution is I don't know
Should we all vacate the town?
Move ourselves to the sticks?
Or stay here and ultimately drown?

Quit our city jobs?
Work in the local pub?
With London rents soaring
We'd be buggered but perhaps we should

For perhaps another
Way we'll find
More conducive to getting
The work-life balance just right

More of the 'me' time
Less of the grind
Space to breathe
De-stress, unwind

For nigh on fifteen hours a week
I traverse this treacherous treadmill
Purely for work, pleasure is extra
And I'm finding it pretty dreadful

So I'm seeking ways
To ease the pain
For I've hit a wall
Can't continue this way

I do have a choice
Though it's a tough one to make
So I'm weighing everything up
For my sanity's at stake

I've done it for the money
But no amount of dosh
Can refund me the hours
Of my life I've lost

So watch this space
We'll see how things pan out
Either poor and sane I'll be
Or loaded with the straitjacket out!

The Beacon

Today I am struggling
But this too shall pass
Today I am low
Ill-tempered, alas

Today I have sunk
And reached a plateau
But the only way is up
No further down shall I go

Yet today I connected
With a familiar voice
Put a face to the kind words
That had given me solace

And this lifted me
Out of myself
It gave me hope
Like casting a spell

A beacon in the darkness
Thus everything seems less bleak
A source of strength
When I was feeling weak.

The Beast Within

Trying to tame
The beast within
When resentment and anger
Surface again

Trying to tame
My acid tongue
When emotions boil over
And the red mist comes

Trying to sit with it
Not spew and vent
Processing so much
Afterwards feeling spent

Wrestling with the urge
To pull the trigger
Unleashing destruction
Entreating something bigger

To intervene
And take the sting away
So that I don't just let rip
And come to regret this day

To pour soothing balm
Over what's spitting inside
So that I may conduct myself
With dignity and pride

Refraining from unleashing
An atomic bomb
Like the old me most certainly
Would have done

Tying myself in knots
Trying to transmute
Rage into compassion
Not recklessly put in the boot

Until finally inspiration
Somehow filters through
Calming the waters
And my fever too

And thus fell they into place
This little collection of words
And my gun was instantly disarmed
And nobody did get hurt.

The Buccaneer

Restless
Sleepless
Wide awake
At this hour

Tossing
Turning
I writhe in bed
Perspire

My mind is racing
Hormonal
And yet
Somehow serene

Having given my will
Over to God
All I can do
Is wait and see

Duvet thrown asunder
I simply stare into space
Something's shifting inside of me
Something's taking place

How beauteous is this state
That I find myself in?
This is what I was yearning for
To feel this way again

My heart's been dormant
For so long
Shattered once
It needed to get strong

So I locked it away
In my treasure chest
Where it gathered dust
And cobwebs

The map I also
Buried deep
But somehow it was discovered
Along with the key

And ever so slowly
Do I now find
That what I thought was dead
Is being coaxed back to life

The current cursing through me
Has jump-started the beat
Of this battered organ
And my blood I can feel reheat

Where it once ran cold
Thus an ice maiden I became
Burning up and thawing out
Etched on my mind his name

The accidental buccaneer
Now a prince in my 'fairy tale'
Yet I care not if the ending is happy
I just care that love does prevail

For I never did expect
To encounter it again
Hence this old heart of mine
Was reluctantly laid to rest

And now am I in heaven
Or perhaps the afterlife
If it's so then let me tell you
It is pure paradise

Thus would I bask here
For eternity, if I might
If not I'll take this moment
Hence why I can't sleep tonight.

The Bull

The bull in the proverbial
China shop
Threw its weight around
In a major strop

Everyone in the vicinity
Ran for cover
Quaking in their boots
Waiting for it to be over

No one understood
What had vexed the bull so
But it literally ran riot
Putting on a real show

Making a spectacle
Of itself
Whilst bystanders trembled
And uneasy felt

No one dared to challenge
This raging animal
They simply walked on eggshells
Feeling vulnerable

Until the storm had passed
And they were no longer in danger
And the bull had calmed down
And was no longer raging

The problem however was
That this was a temporary reprieve
The bull was a repeat offender
Though still permitted to roam free

Which baffled many
Who couldn't understand
Why no one did
The bull reprimand

But this was a wild beast
So could not be 'civilised'
Could not undergo anger management
Like, perhaps, you and I

So why let it loose
In a public place?
If it couldn't be taught
The error of its ways?

Perhaps it had escaped
And now couldn't be caught
But its antics certainly were
Food for thought

The sight of that bull
Out of control
The way it made people feel
Was a lesson to behold

It wasn't pretty viewing
Everyone was a wreck
And many of them vowed
Themselves to protect

By staying away from the bull
And the china shop
Indefinitely
If it could not be stopped.

The Bungling Telephonist

I once did a very ditsy thing
Live on national TV
Lived up to my blonde highlights
For all the viewers to see

Talking Telephone Numbers
Was in question the game
And in massively screwing up
I almost made my name

Wracked with intense stage fright
At busting my cherry on telly
I royally f**ked up
And my pants got really smelly

I made an expensive mistake
When answering the phones
On what was a rollover week
Crowning the first 'winner' of this new show

Twenty Thousand Smackers
Given to the wrong bloke
All that lovely dosh
Veritably up in smoke!

Now the notorious
Number 85
Was living in peril
Fearing being skinned alive

No choice but to fess up
To Mr Celador, Paul Smith
The producer and creator
An important man, no s**t!

I was quaking in my platforms
When I gingerly pulled him aside
Fearing that I'd be given
For sure my P45

But instead he stifled a giggle
Told my eighteen-year-old self he knew
Told me not to be afraid
And that Schoey would forgive me too!

Told me to take it to my grave
And do my very best
To never ever tell a soul
But some b*****d leaked it to the press!

I had to go into hiding
I did a very good job
They never tracked me down
Though they tried and failed, thank God

And the saga made it into 'Bizarre'
The column in *The Sun*
As written by Andy Coulson
Who ribbed me like a good 'un

Deemed me 'The Bungling Telephonist'
Brainless between the ears
Notwithstanding the fact
The beneficiary was now rich but 'in tears'

Said he couldn't enjoy
His winnings knowing it was a blunder
So he's pictured cracking open the champers
With a face semi-smug yet like thunder!

And what of I?
Number 85?
How did things pan out for me?

Well I kept my trap shut
(Until now at least)
But Schoey never did forgive me.

The Crush Of Capitalism

Are we all but slaves
Hamsters on a wheel
Paid to run on a treadmill
That barely stands still?

Pounding away
Day in and day out
With our noses to the grindstone
Our spirits almost snuffed out?

Striving hard to keep
A roof over our heads
And provide for ourselves
Lest the streets become our beds?

The cost of living rises
Yet wages still stagnate
The ever-moving goalposts
That stretch us 'til we break

Capitalism thrives
Its machinery fuelled by greed
It chews you up and spits you out
Takes no prisoners, no reprieve

Perhaps it's time to surrender
To bow out of the game
You gave it your best shot
But your sanity's at stake

You want to live a little
Before you grow too old
You want to hold something back
Not sell your very soul

You've given it your all
But that was not enough
Time to cut your losses
It shouldn't be this tough

You were born free
Not wearing a ball and chain
We all should work to live
Not live to work – it's insane!

Not mortgage ourselves to the hilt
And commit to it for life
We shouldn't have to pay
For basic human rights

And don't get me started on rent
Oh, pity the poor tenant
Held to ransom by landlords
Who prey on the dire situation

We'll all be residing in boxes
Nay, coffins at this rate
Prices need to be capped
Before it gets too late

Before they bring back the workhouse
And incarcerate us there
For it seems that's where we're heading
With social housing so scarce

I just want to be happy
To have enough to eat
I really can't be arsed
With all this sh*t to compete

Just want to be warm and dry
Comfy in my bed
Just want a place to call home
Somewhere to rest my head

And the time to create and dream
To express myself and write
In a sanctuary of my own
Where I know I'm safe at night

With someone to snuggle up to
And share the 'joys' of this world
Just simple pleasures really
That shouldn't cost the earth.

The Eye In The Sky

The all-seeing Eye of London
Now dominates Waterloo sky
Towering above Big Ben
Even Westminster seems shy

What secrets has it beheld?
What knowledge does it keep?
Illuminated, illuminati-like
Almost never do you sleep

Like the Wheel of Fortune
Or the hands of time do you turn
Spinning like the earth on its axis
Watchful, you look and learn.

The Falling Tower

Supermarkets
Are out of stock
All fresh food gone
Because the 'herd' ran amok

Nothing left
But junk and sweets
Because some greedy idiots
Only themselves thought to please

Bring back rationing!
At least make the game fair!
We all have to eat!
And can't survive on fresh air!

Gluttony is one
Of the Seven Deadly Sins
Greed another
Yet the mayhem begins

How savage we become
As depicted in *Lord Of The Flies*
When the masses lose the plot
And society disintegrates before our eyes

And what of our government?
Suspending mortgages but not rent?
How is that equality?
What kind of message does that send?

Why are homeowners protected?
But the rest of us exposed?
Condemned to possible eviction?
If the economy implodes?

Do they want the poorer amongst us?
Out on the streets?
Begging for mercy?
'Til we succumb to the disease?

Then consider the NHS staff
Fighting this war
Without adequate equipment
Or protective uniforms!

Working on the frontline
Tackling the virus
Then abandoned at home
If they become victims of the crisis

GP surgeries have closed
We're told to dial 111
But the line's permanently engaged
We can't talk to anyone

So those who have symptoms
Quarantine in despair
Because no one will test them
To confirm/allay their worst fears

Forced to ride it out
Wondering whether they'll pull through
Whilst politicians declare
20,000 deaths a GOOD result!

How is that GOOD?!
Do they mean to say that's the TARGET?!
Are they AIMING for 20,000 PEOPLE
To actually cark it?

How callous a statement
So devoid of compassion
Fanning the flames of terror
When what is required is action

The lunatics are running
This veritable asylum
The sane seem to be in the minority
Amid all this pandemonium

I understand the desire
To evacuate into space
Flee a zillion light years away
From this God-forsaken place

That said I still have faith
That our serenity will be restored
And I'm down on my knees
Praying for everyone of us

For before the calm
Inevitably comes the storm
Cleansing and purging
Though the thunder roars

The rain may fall
Torrentially
But this could be the catalyst
That ultimately sets us free

As all that was hidden
Now comes to light
The stark reality
Of a world in plight

A 'civilisation' so sick
It will ultimately destroy itself
Toppling the few
Who currently hoard global wealth

Because this living nightmare
Is forcing the sleeping to wake up
The revolution is coming
The Falling Tower has been struck.

The Hopeful Spinster

The sun sets on her youth
Bereft of her luscious leaves
She approaches the autumn of her life
Convinced of what she believes

Barren now
A starless sky
Save for that glimmer
In her eye

Of hope that soon
He'll arrive
She waits for him quietly
For when the planets align

United they'll forever be
Never will it be the same
When he appears finally
This lady and her twin flame.

The Hunger Games

Should I become vegan?
Or should I become veggie?
Or maybe pescatarian?
The possibilities make me edgy

Everyone you ask
Tells you something different
It seems all food is bad
That's the only thing that's consistent

Don't eat dairy
Don't eat meat
Don't eat soya
Don't eat wheat

Oats are bad
All cereals are junk
Nuts can be lethal
Pulses gunk

Have sugar at your peril
It truly is the devil
Avoid alcohol at all costs
Even fructose can get lost!

Caffeine is totally out
As if you were in any doubt
Just water or herbal tea
As you feel yourself stifling a scream!!!

Fill up on probiotics
Powders, potions, tinctures and tonics
If you want to be bionic
Deprivation is key so get on it!

And ensure that what you buy
Is organic or you will fry
In hell (aren't you in there already?)
As these rules render you batty and unsteady

In the supermarket
You're deranged
Everything's toxic
You go insane

Scrutinising the labels
But the print's so f**king tiny
You can't decipher it with glasses
Alas, you give up trying

And all the while you're ravenous
About to eat your own face
You need some sustenance now!
A café seems the sensible place

But then you become that person
Who's totally and utterly neurotic
That gives the poor waiter a migraine
Because the menu has nothing on it

That you are permitted to have
On your restrictive diet
Unless the chef takes extreme measures
To cater for your preposterous requirements

Like he has the time!
Or really can be arsed!
His blood pressure must be sky high!
It's absurd beyond a farce!

What to do?
I hear you exclaim?!
Literally EVERYTHING'S forbidden
Please someone explain!

What's happening to the world?
I reluctantly admit defeat
I'm exasperated, nigh emaciated
Can't practise what they preach!

Are the food police truly, really
So holier than thou?
Do they honestly rigidly stick
To such regimes – I mean tell me HOW?!

They surely can't be human
They must be undercover ETs
They mustn't have work to do
They certainly DON'T f**king eat!

Is this horse sh*t really a ploy?
By them to exterminate us all?
For they'll wipe us out, I have no doubt
Unless we them can foil

They're traumatising us to the point
That we're all nearly foodophobic
Soon we'll only dare to consume fresh air
And eventually expire from it

Beyond anorexic
Bulimic and such
A pandemic of eating disorders
It really is too much

Don't listen (unless you're allergic)!
Devour what you like!
Screw the consequences!
Tell them all to take a hike!

Ignore this flaming baloney!
In your arse it's a royal pain!
And leave the malnourished 'Martians'
To their heinous hunger games.

The Invisible Assassin

And the lockdown was rolled out
Like an incoming tsunami's tide
Incremental waves of restriction
Engulfed our liberty in a sea of spies

Unprecedented surveillance
Even civilians named and shamed
As society gradually fractured
Whilst its very foundations did shake

The invisible assassin
Unleashed knew no bounds
Airborne and ultimately deadly
Like wildfire it spread around

The people were petrified
Into desperate submission
They cried out to the powers-that-be
And demanded a solution

To be protected
By the state
Thus a totalitarian system
Was being put in place

Global house arrest
The unprecedented measure taken
Forced to segregate
They dwelt in self-isolation

For how long
Could not be said
But this was preferable
If it protected them from death

And so they obeyed
And did as instructed
Barely challenging
Announcements from the 'pulpit'

At this time of uncertainty
Others kept heightened emotions in check
Entreated their loved ones to inhale the light
And though anxious be circumspect

"Let go of fear but be vigilant
"Human rights are being eroded
"Let us not get complacent
"About laws which to democracy are corrosive

"Question everything
"And as and when this has passed
"Demand again that these draconian rules
"Are completely and utterly rolled back"

For the invisible assassin
May indeed advance far and wide
But the implications for our future freedom
Need to be temporary and justified.

The Key

When your peace of mind
Is shattered to bits
And you worry about everything

When little things
Really get on your t**s
And you're anxious about what tomorrow will bring

When you dread getting up
And facing the day
And your stomach is tied up in knots

When you question your sanity
Along the way
And you feel like you've lost your guts

Search within, go deep inside
Connect with your centre
With your arms open wide

Seek tranquility
And your own inner peace
Soothe yourself when your strength is weak

Find that distant
Chink of light in the dark
Like the star of Bethlehem

Follow its lead
'Til it lights up your heart
And your inner voice finally begins to sing

Immerse yourself
In that which you love
Retreat into your protective shell

Batten down the hatches
Convene with your soul
And perhaps with the angels as well

No one is alone in this universe
No matter how it may feel
No matter how you may hurt

The Divine belongs
To one and all
And is there for the taking, if you will

We all are cherished
Even when we fall
No one is condemned to hell

So breathe, my friend,
Inhale deeply the light
Feel its radiance replenish and restore

Learn your worth
Stand up and fight
Love thyself a little more

Have faith in YOU
And Heaven above
And go knock, knock, knocking on its gate

You have the key
To open that door
Do it now – don't hesitate!

The Littlest Star

The sun and the moon
Had a terrible fight
The petrified stars
Could not shine that night

A thunderstorm
With lightning bolts
Because the sun got mad
His rays red-hot

He burnt the moon
And thus the moon waned
One of the stars
Supernova'd away

The littlest star
Got caught in between
But she was too small
To intervene

She shone close to the moon
So the moon could wax
But the moon couldn't maintain
Its light and collapsed

Into a crescent
Barely there and dim
And then the moon fled
From the sun and hid

The littlest star panicked
Twinkled as brightly as she could
An SOS
To the celestial neighbourhood

Finally an Angel
Answered her call
And the littlest star
Explained it all

The Angel told her
She must speak to God
Only He could prevent
A catastrophic flood

So the littlest star
Prayed to Him
And He agreed
He needed to step in

To ascertain why
The sun burst into flames
Was he bewitched?
Possessed? Deranged?

And he summoned the sun
To the planet Mars
To stand before Him
And be judged for the scars

He'd inflicted on the moon
To be held to account
To establish what
It was all about

The moon went mute
She was afraid of the sun
Only the littlest star
Could reveal what happened

But what a monumental task
Before God to stand
And expose the sun
For his heavy hand

Alas, the littlest star
Innately could not lie
She'd witnessed the sun's antics
As he'd dominated the sky

She too had been scorched
By several of his flares
But of the consequences of testifying
She was scared

She was caught between
A rock and a hard place
Torn in two
She felt she might break

The burden was heavy
She couldn't help but cry
She had no one to lean on
But she had to do what was right

As the Day drew nearer
She tried to gather strength
God was determined
The sun would repent

And thus the clock ticks
The sand trickles through the glass
As they all wait on tenterhooks
For justice to be passed.

The MADina

Marrakech, Morocco
The mayhem of the Médina
If you catch anybody's eye
It will cost you much in dirham

Empty pockets
Outstretched hands
Abject poverty
In this barren, desert land

The dust and the dirt
The drought and dilapidation
You wander through the labyrinth
Confused but with heightened sensation

The frenzied streets
Pulse rapidly with traffic
Rudiment'ry modes of transport
Compete for space, direction erratic

Cars, mopeds, bikes, horses and donkeys
Darting all around you
Knocking you off-course
Making you wonky

A flock of chickens
Pecking at your feet
As you peruse the trinkets
And the million artisans' treats

Pungent aromas
Permeate the air
As you battle the persistent onslaught
Of beggars everywhere

Souvenirs aplenty
They want you to take them all home
Your wish is their command
As you stare and aimlessly roam

Eventually lost
Defeated by the maze
You seek to leave the souk
That by now has you severely dazed

Helped by 'Fatima's' hand
In Limona you find shelter
A welcome, familiar haunt
Shaded to cool your swelter

You rest there for a while
Recover from the ordeal
Of arriving in a land
So alien and unreal

A taste of something exotic
You've never before encountered
Culture shock a grenade to your mind
At the foot of the Atlas Mountains

You gladly drink the wine
Given freely for your nerves
That by now are shot to bits
In this place that you traverse

The kindness of these strangers
A needed comfort at last
The pace finally slowing down
After starting supersonically fast

You eventually wend your way
To the sanctuary of the riad
An oasis in the eye of the storm
A place to unwind and find peace

Tomorrow is another day
A new adventure to behold
It's what you signed up for, after all:
An awakening for the soul.

The Money-Go-Round

The merry-go-round of money
The things that people do!
It all comes down to money
It sucks but this is true

Everything has a fee
And it costs just to be alive
From cradle to grave we consume
And even basic needs have a price

The clothes we wear
The water we drink
The food we eat
The kitchen sink

The travel to work
The roof over our heads
Entertainment and hobbies
Thus we spin in our beds

It's all a bloody madness
This ebb and flow of cash
It can make or break civilisations
Cause suicides, murder en mass

Wars are fought
And crimes committed
People seduced
Jailed, embittered

Gambling's rife
If you don't have enough
Some win, some lose
For this game's really tough

This roller coaster ride
The currency of life
Makes you high, makes you low
Makes you have sleepless nights

So unpredictable
You celebrate or seethe
Everything is taxed
Save the air that we breathe

But with all the pollution
Surely it's only a matter of time
Before they take ownership of that
And sell it back to us 'cleansed' of grime!

You have to laugh
You really do
Having to pay to wipe your arse
When you go to the loo?!

Even bog roll ain't free
As aren't tampons and the like
And every financial year
Do they the prices hike

The 'cost of living'
Ever rising with inflation
The powers-that-be
A veritable conflagulation

"Spend your money!
"Sell your incarnation!
"Work to earn a crust!"
They preach with exultation

Then when you're old and grey
And totally clapped out
You finally kick the bucket
And they charge you to be thrown out!

Oh, how my blonde mind boggles
It really doesn't make sense
The way this silly world quibbles
Over every pound and pence

Eradicate the stuff!
It's evil, do say I!
Surely we were born to dance
Not to barter, sell and buy!

Everything we need
Was given to us by 'God'
So how can you put a price on this Earth?
And its contents, you silly sod?

Did you create this land?
The animals, plants and trees?
The sun and sky above?
The oceans, lakes and streams?

Of course you didn't, you prat
But you've claimed it for your own
And now you preside over it
From upon your gilded throne

Well a throne is but a perch
And can be fallen off
And one day I hope you're toppled
If enough of us get cross!

The Naked Flame

I gaze into
The naked flame
Transfixed
I watch it burn

Flickering
It glows before me
My weary soul
Yearns

For something beyond
This 'reality'
So tangible yet
It cannot be seen

That I desperately seek
Knowing it will fulfil me
Though some might say
It's a dream

The naked flame
So mesmerising
Almost caressing my face
As it moves

The warming heat
It radiates
I soften, entranced
And soothed

My mind's eye widens
The vortex gapes
Illuminated
I begin to escape

From the shackles
Of the physical
Senses heightened
The metaphysical

Into the realms
Of the mystical world
Where questions are answered
And mysteries unfurled

Where celestial voices
Whisper their wisdom
To those who are attuned
And possess the vision

Who have the wherewithal
To boldly venture
Between dimensions
Who in the past were censured

The wizards and witches
The sorcerers and priests
The high priestesses, gods and goddesses
The Ancient Egyptians and Greeks

I stay awhile
And play with fire
To be an initiate
Is my heart's desire.

The Nightmare Before Christmas

Whether you vote Tory
Or whether you vote Labour
Whether you abstain
From using that piece of paper

Keep it under you hat
Because to publicise it will just inflame
The deliberately divisive debates
That are nothing but a game

For divided we fall
And united we stand
For divide and rule
Is the ultimate plan

Split the country
Down the middle
Blame each other
For the Brexit fiddle

Get the general public
At each other's throats
Then for the competing parties
Expect them all to vote

Get them all to trudge
To the polling stations
Right on top of Christmas
Fanning the flames of a confused nation

At what should be
A time of peace
So many heightened emotions
So much unrest and unease

Let's all talk manifestos
Instead of goodwill to the world
Let's see our 'leaders' at loggerheads
And rage against the machine unfurl

Let's whip the country
Into a frenzy
To hell with seasonal cheer
Give 'em politics aplenty!

And overshadow what should be
The happiest time of the year
A time to lay down arms
A time to forget our fears

Yes, deprive them of that
Give them much to worry about
Get spinning that spin, ye doctors
Get them soapboxes out!

Bring out the boxing gloves
Play dirty, certainly don't play fair
Crack on with the smear campaigns
Don't even come up for air!

And put Brexit in prime position
The burning 'star' atop the tree
The catalyst for everything
Threatening to end democracy

What a brilliant idea –
Whitehall, you shouldn't have!
To hell with the birth of Christ
The PM's job is up for grabs!

And so instead of celebrating
We all engage in our various campaigns
Perhaps set ourselves up for a fall
If we have our hearts set on who 'wins'

But if someone 'wins'
Someone always will lose
And we really should be as one
Not divided and having to choose

So, like I said, keep schtum
If indeed do this we must
Then get on with having fun
And commemorating Christmas.
#generalelection2019

The Patriarch

Why is it always a war zone
Whenever we're in the same room?
The words you hurl cut like a knife
Jagged edges rip through me and wound

Lacerations so deep
I will never recover
They tear in to my very soul

Thought at least
You'd mellow with age
But the venom's still there now you're old

I run away
In pieces again
Torn apart by the things you've said

It shatters my heart
Every single time
As the onslaught resounds in my head

And Christmas is always
The worst time of all
Seems you store it all up for that

A pressure cooker
Of bitterness
Then you blow and go on the attack

Annihilating everyone
You somehow claim to love
Gunning them down with vitriol
Remorselessly spilling their blood

And then you wonder
Why you're alone
Save for one you've managed to shackle

A hostage no less
In a prison of fear
Subjugated, down-trodden from the battle

A life sentence it seems
For all concerned
Blurred lines t'ween the present and past

Unforgiving
Eternally
Seems you'll rage 'til you breathe your last

And what of this 'child'
You claim to cherish
Who you repeatedly drive from her 'home'?

Disconnecting her
From her family
So that she has to suffer and roam?

I will never understand you
And will always lament
That you were given to me

Try as I might
A silver lining to find
Thus far it's impossible to see.

The Raucous Rooster

There once was a raucous rooster
That let rip from dusk 'til dawn
Squawking and squeaking
Shattering the silence
Wailing at and waking everyone

Atop the riad's roof
In its un-soundproofed coop
Lived the little s**t

Safe as houses
Out of reach
Where the likes of us couldn't get at it

On the hour
Every hour
Its creaky cries could be heard

Sharp enough
To shatter glass
This was no sweet songbird

So out of tune
It serenaded the moon
Its croaky chords sending shockwaves into space

I'll never know
How us occupants below
Got any shuteye with that cock on our case

Oh how we fantasised
Oh how we dreamed
Of wringing its neck
And rendering it tagine

If only to get
A bit of peace
Instead of tossing and turning
And counting bloody sheep

And its feathers could have been dyed
And arranged into a sphere
A Juju Hat to be wall-mounted
Like the prized head of a deer

That we had hunted and felled
In an insomnia-induced frenzy
By commandeering an earth-to-air missile
For a few thousand dirham and twenty

And launching it at
That f**king coop
Where the raucous rooster reigned supreme

Atop the riad's roof in Essauria
A fishing port
On the edge of the Medine.

The Road

Catapulted into the world
My journey began
A life unfurled

The road ahead was long
I embarked on a path
I'm not sure I planned to be on

I managed to somehow crawl
Began to walk
Sometimes I'd fall

I'd have to get back up
My legs were unsteady
To stand was tough

But I got there in the end
Skills for the future
Had I learned

Obstacles come and go
Humpback bridges
Jar the flow

The potholes can catch me out
Stumbling
Sometimes I cry out

Sometimes it's plain sailing
I bound along
Without complaining

Sometimes I have a hand to hold
To keep me company
And contemplate growing old

Sometimes I go it alone
The littlest hobo
Needing no one

Other times I yearn for a friend
But ultimately
We negotiate the bends

And twists and turns by ourselves
For it's a solo trip
That cannot be shelved.

The Saga Of The Salmon

There was only one salmon
Left in the shop
On Christmas Eve
When to home I got

I wanted a side
But this one was whole
That said we were three
So around it could go

The price was a bargain
Only twenty quid
So we decided to grab it
Before someone else did

I kindly asked the fishmonger
To work his magic
To gut it and section it
But his craftsmanship was tragic

He cleaned out its insides
Then left it at that
Slid its poor carcass
Into a placky bag

That wasn't even sealed
And it was sliding around
When I clocked it I was livid
And gave him a dressing down

"What have you done?!
"What an abortion!
"Is that your idea
"Of filleted salmon portions?

"It's as long as I'm tall
"In one massive piece
"I'd envisioned beautiful steaks
"And two sides at least

"But that cock-up looks like
"You've both had a fight
"And that the unfortunate salmon
"Came back to life

"And fought until the end
"Whilst you brandished your blade
"Which must have been serrated
"Judging by the mess you've made!

"It's got jagged edges
"All torn to shreds
"And by the look of those fins
"You haven't removed its legs

"The width isn't even
"It's triangle-shaped
"And it's a metre in length
"You've clearly made a mistake!"

Turns out he was
A Christmas temp
Not a trained fishmonger
And wanted his break

So he rushed and fled
Leaving a mess
So I had to call his manager
And flaming protest

Who was horrified
When he saw the state
Of the poor salmon
Unfit for a plate

He ordered the temp
To finish the job
And I had to direct
The inexperienced poor sod

Like I know how to prep
A whopping great fish?!
But back in Crouch End
There'd have been none of this

They're all fully qualified
To do the job
Take pride in their work
Though it costs a few bob

But the end result
Is a thing of beauty
All precise and portioned
And packaged and pretty

Not all mangled up
In a slimy bag
That it takes two people to haul
And yank and drag

But we got there in the end
By the skin of our teeth
And the unfortunate salmon
Looked more palatable at least

And they gave us a discount
Which can't be bad
So I summoned some Christmas spirit
And forgave the poor lad

Then headed home
To see my folks
Brandishing said salmon
The poor butt of the joke

But we gave it a fitting
Send off in the end
Baked it with lemon
'Til it was fit for a king

So all was not lost
And it gave us a giggle
Breaking the ice
And filling our middles

It literally was
The catch of the day
And it tasted delicious
I'm happy to say.

The Sting

Sub-zero temperatures
Falling snow
Outside seeming
Not a great place to go

Tucked up in bed
Electric blanket on
Huddled under the duvet
Waiting for the sun to come

This winter has
A sting in its tail
Spring struggling to burst out
Feeling tired and frail

Burrowing down
Keeping warm
Sleep descends
I hibernate some more

Nights are pulling out
But still the darkness is long
All consuming it envelops
Subduing vitality and song

Protracted coldness
Bites and snaps
Icy winds
Whip and slap

Akin to an assault
If one should venture into the street
Exposing oneself to the elements
In a bid to make ends meet

But lucky are those
With a roof over their heads
Some bed down on pavements
No shelter save for their threads

A sickening injustice
In this day and age
More poignant now than ever
I feel my weary heart break.

The 'Therapist'

Utterly irresponsibly
You opened a can of worms
This bollocks that you call CBT
Has left me scarred and burned

You lifted the lid
On my darkest times
Then ejected me back
Into the wild

You said you could assist
But instead you just drew
Pathetic diagrams
After I my guts had spewed

You then said we only had ten
Sessions – this was not your field
But there I was exposed
My wounds now open not healed

Well thanks very much
For being so out of touch
For creating a ticking bomb
That might go off – for I can't carry on

Like this anymore
I am on the proverbial floor
And you are the catalyst
That has made me feel like this

I'll find a way out
For a survivor am I
I'll get my shit together
And my tears will dry

But reader be wary
Of 'therapists'
That will take your money
Then cast you adrift

Maybe it's better
To work through it yourself
You've done it before
It's called self-help.

The Voice Of The Soul

Listen to your feelings
Your soul is speaking to you
Sending a message loud and clear
Guiding you towards your truth

If you remember how to speak its language
You'll understand what its trying to convey
You'll have the resources within you
To hear all it has to say.

The Volatile Vegan

A volatile vegan
Abused me today
I have nothing against vegans
Unless they rain on my parade

This volatile vegan
Clever thought she were
When she grabbed me by my collar
To check it if it was fur

Upon deciding it was
She regarded me with disgust
Let go like it was on fire
And strutted off proud of what she had 'sussed'

Her eyes literally filled
With vitriol
She spun on her heel
After piercing my soul

The silent venom
She injected me with
Could melt lead into liquid
Even with just one drip

I was made to feel
Like I'd skinned something alive
In actual cold blood
Then worn it with pride

I wouldn't mind
But this actually happened
Not near a PETA protest
But at work in Stratford

Extreme behaviour
That was utterly out of place
Judgemental and self-righteous
And totally in my face

If you are vehemently vegan
Don't inflict your views on me
Your beliefs belong to you
And don't give you the right to preach

How dare you actually
Invade my personal space?
Grab hold of my clothing
Pass judgement, radiate hate?

Look down on me
With intense disdain
Act satisfied and smug
That you've inflicted pain?

You ought to be ashamed
Yet you take the moral high ground
Thank God I'm not like you
A condescending b***h with an axe to grind.

The Wheel

Broken once
Boundaries shattered
Faith destroyed
Nothing mattered

Nothing to live for
Estranged from God
Hopeless and abandoned
Cast out, unloved

A lifeline offered
With a price tag
She took it all the same
It was all she had

And for a while
It served its purpose
Alleviating the loneliness
But it made her nervous

Off the beaten
Track was she
In uncharted waters
Albeit set free

Free to live
And love again
A lighter heart
Anaesthetising pain

But this road was perilous
And the further she went
Into the enchanted forest
Did she begin to repent

But the Wolf Moon then rose
'Twas the witching hour
Suddenly she was possessed
Deprived of her willpower

She succumbed to the demon
All hell broke loose
And when dawn broke
The awful truth

She was caught in a vice
No seeming way out
Only back into that pit
She not so long had climbed out

Oh Lord, what to do?
Then she heard His voice
A small word in her ear
A whisper, a barely audible noise

A call to arms
Which she acted upon
Just one syllable
But like firing a gun

This shot in the dark
Was all she had
When all was at stake
And she was woefully sad

Gripped with fear
And frustration
In a maze
No sense of salvation

Suddenly hope was restored
And she grabbed it with both hands
Prayed for a solution
And He obliged with a plan

Thus the Wheel of Fortune
Turned in her favour
And she was reconnected
With her Saviour.

The World

Peeling back the layers
Wondering who I am
Evaluating everything
Ascertaining what is a sham

Digging deep within
Listening to the call of my soul
It's screaming at me to do something
Yet what I don't actually know

Clearly I've been exasperated
Entrapped by circumstance
Literally dying to free myself
Given half a chance

The road ahead is uncertain
Not sure which direction to take
But treading water isn't working
And I feel it's make or break

If I stagnate I'll surely go mad
I'm already borderline there
Monumentally overburdened
Not of myself taking care

But rather soldiering on
Like a snow plough through a blizzard
Churning through great walls of ice
In dire need of a Wizard

Who'll wave a magic wand
And make all my dreams come true
So that I can find respite
From what I've been putting myself through

For nobody made me
Make the choices I made
Though some perhaps influenced
The fact that I've stayed

For so long
In an ill-fitting place
Climbing a mountain
Too vast to negotiate

Trying to stay afloat
On an infinite, untamed ocean
That tosses me this way and that
And is constantly in motion

Clinging on for dear life
To the raft that I commandeered
Terrified of the water
Which never before have I feared

I used to just take the plunge
Without ever thinking twice
Run and jump just like that!
Almost taking flight

I saw it as an adventure
A thrilling dip on this roller coaster ride
Exhilarating though my heart was in my mouth
No intention of suicide

But that was when I was young
And fearless and naïve
That was when I had 'the balls'
And unlimited energy

Older now
I proceed with caution
Wary of pitfalls
Intuition distorted

Having had my faith shaken
I almost struggle to trust
But they're urging me onwards
And I must be robust

For if I don't do
What I know I must
They'll force me somehow
And that could be tough

Best it's my decision
To make that change
Take that chance
And not hesitate

Best I follow
My heart and my head
Which now are in tandem
I just need the strength

To board that Chariot
And take the reigns
Steer my course
And not remain

In this situation
I've found myself in
It's time to say adieu
And begin again

Start from scratch
For this cycle has almost played out
As confirmed by The World card
Which has left me in no doubt.

Tightrope

Revealing
Feelings
Necessary
But never easy

Throws you
You lose control
For he knows you
Vulnerable

Yet wonderful
Release
Retention
Intolerable

Out there
Loud and clear
He 'sees' you
You have no fear

Now what?
Oh my God!
On a tightrope
Of does he, does he not

Feel the same
Want to play this game
Who knows...
...watch this space.

Time On Their Hands

The calm after the storm
The waters have stilled
Time for reflection
Time to be filled

Too much time for some
Weighing heavily on their hands
A novel thing but unwelcome
As they wish they had more plans

Time together
Dramatic and fraught
Sped by, yes,
But them it overwrought

Yet they yearn for this time
As separated they are bereft
Unable to live apart
Unable thus to rest

The solution elusive
The outcome unknown
What to do for the best?
Best leave them alone.

Timing

Timing truly is everything
And for me the time is now
No time like the present
I'd forgotten that somehow

Been waiting for this moment
And now it has arrived
I'm surfing the crest of a wave
Experiencing sheer delight

Don't put off until tomorrow
What you can do today
Seize the opportunities
That providence sends your way!

Tired But Wired

Oh dear, have I messed up!
Caffeined to the max
Four double macchiatos and an Irish coffee
I fear a heart attack!

Supposed to be getting an early night
But I'm wired to the moon
Charged like a Duracell battery
I'm such a dizzy spoon

With the weather so dreary
And me so glum
I drowned my sorrows
In several coffee cups

Trying to lift
My heavy spirits
Sans alcohol
But I'm over the limit

My head is buzzing
And kinda hurts
I twitch and sweat
At times I jerk

What to do?
On a Wednesday
With all this pizazz
That is here to stay

Can't exactly party
When I'm up at the crack of dawn
And when I'm on a detox
And I'd planned to be alone

Is there an antidote?
A sedative I can take?
Or shall I go for a ten-hour hike
And resign myself to staying awake?

Now I've heard that Red Bull
Gives you wings
But this is pure rocket fuel
Designed for orbit and space and things

Not what you need
When you've a big day ahead
And what you should really be doing
Is snuggling up sleeping in bed!

'Tis The Season...

December descends
Advent begins
Tinsel is hung
Jingle bells ring

Small children dream
Of Santa Claus
Big children party
Wine is poured

The days shorter now
Dark winter nights
Trees are decorated
Adorned with lights

Gifts are wrapped
Cards are sent
Rich food is eaten
Much money is spent

Somewhere in the mayhem
The real message is hidden
Frankie touched upon it
When 'The Power Of Love' was written

It captures the true essence
Of what it means to me
A sentiment that can be lost
In the consumerism and frivolity

A time to turn within
To reconnect with source
A time to process the waning year
Release it without remorse

A time to make amends
And turn over a new, blank page
And prepare to write the next chapter
A time to begin again.

To My Fallen Fellows

No one's judging you
We know you're not weak
You're just suffering from
A terrible disease

We just love you
We all care
We want to help you
We want to be there

To bring you back
From the brink
None of us want
Your ship to sink

You are beautiful
You are kind
So vivacious
When your spirit shines

You are needed
We miss you so
Know that we are here for you
Know you're not alone

Please pick up the phone
Please reply to our texts
Please open up the door
We just want to protect

You from your demons
You were doing so well
But this situation
We know is a living hell

Please reach out
Make a call
To any of us
We'll catch you before you fall

Don't give up
Stop while you still can
We entreat you to be courageous
And accept our outstretched hands!

Torn

Is the end nigh?
I fear for you
I grieve
I cry

I worry you're going to leave
And how I'm going to cope
Your pallor is grey, you're weary
And why I do not know

I wish I could make you better
But I don't know where to start
I love you more than you know
You're embedded in my heart

You've been here my whole life
I've never known a world without you
If this is it then give me strength
To be there and see you through

Watching you suffer this way
Tears me totally apart
I go for I can't bear to stay
And watch you drift, depart

On tenterhooks we wait
For the outcome of your tests
I gave you the only gift I could
The return of the one you love best

Hoping together
You'll find a way
To face what's in store
And celebrate

The time you have left
For I fear it is little
Thus it is precious
Though weak and brittle

Make the most of it, please
Put your weapons down
Call a truce
The time is now.

Traumas At Toni & Cry

Hair-raising times
At Toni & Guy
Went in for highlights
But now I could cry

They persuaded me to go
For a whole new look
"Try balayage!"
But they totally f**ked it up

Now it's gone all sludgy
With lashings of mud and grey
They left me bloody speechless
But what the heck could I say?

They saw my face
I was mortified
Though I stifled my tears
I could've really cried

"Come back next week!
"We'll bleach it, make it right"!
But how do you trust
A crimper that's sh*te?

They said he was the best
In the whole salon
Well, he must be colour-blind
He got it so wrong!

I legged it out the door
Down to Terror Sorbie
They plied me with Prosecco
When they heard my horror story

Said that they could fix it
For £350 quid!
So I downed another glass
Then fled and bloody hid

I've never liked the mop shop
Had so many disasters
It's worse than going to the dentist –
I'm raging in the rafters!

Sobbing into my soup
Wearing a beanie hat
I can never take it off
Or go out and that's a fact!

So I'm going to retire
And become a proper recluse
Until I'm old and bald
And no longer have hair to do.

Travelling Traumas

Packing to go away
The bane of my life
A middle-class disaster
Causing me untold strife

Clothes strewn asunder
Can't see the floor
The bed nor the chair
Can't even open the door

What outfits to take?
How many pairs of shoes?
Can I live without my protein spray?
Straighteners and mousse?

Toiletries weigh a ton
Perfume and deo too
Haven't packed my undies yet
And conditioner and shampoo

My chum will be lucky –
We're sharing a case
But what with the kitchen sink
There's barely any space!

She stipulated ketchup
And I reckon maybe if I'm clever
I can squeeze in some sachets
But a whole bottle? Never

We split the extortionate cost
Of taking proper luggage
Almost the price of the ticket
What a load of rubbish

However it seems
She's due a rebate
I'll never fill just half
At this bloody rate

Just can't travel light
I'm a freaking nightmare
Ten flaming kilos
Just on products for my hair!

Then there's the slap
Jewellery and slippers
And don't get me started
On the spare pairs of knickers

A skip would be more apt
And a truck to transport
Fingers crossed the plane takes off
With all this crap that I've brought

Clothes are an impediment
When you're a kleptomaniac like this
Next time I'll holiday in a nudist camp
And bugger the baggage – what bliss!

Tremors

My very foundations are shaken
The earth tremors beneath my feet
The world around me seems unsafe and insecure
And thus do I not sleep

The tectonic plates have shifted
Causing a rift deep inside the seabed
It feels like a tsunami is building
On the horizon a huge wave rears its head

The walls of my haven start to crumble
Shuddering with all the strain
I brace myself for certain impact
The Falling Tower at play again

The shackles that bind me are breaking apart
And like a shuttle re-entering earth's atmosphere
I wonder if I can withstand the force
Of the prospective annihilation I fear

All I can do is batten down the hatches
And ensure that my faith is strong
For no one can predict how this will end
It's out of my hands and in God's.

Tug Of 'Love'

The tug of 'love'
Or rather tug-of-war
Under the thumb
His temper flares

He sees the red mist
She disobeyed
He clenches his fists
In a white-hot rage

She argues back
He tries to silence
But he'll never admit
He's prone to violence

'She winds him up'
Or so he says
'They're all mentally ill'
'He's the one who's sane'

She's out the door
He yells in the street
In fast pursuit
As she tries to flee

But his claws are embedded
Deep in her psyche
Ingrained for decades
And she just can't fight it

'He didn't do it'
'She made it up'
So on it goes
This tug of 'love'

He won't confess
Even to himself
Thus it continues
As he refuses help

Thus like a yo-yo
He yanks her back in
And spins her in his lies
Until she's bound up in string

There's no escape
Alas, it seems
A fight to death?
Is that the key?

The cavalry has been
Time and time again
But time and time again
Neither will relent

Embroiled in this saga
For all to see
Until one of them succumbs
To their own mortality.

Unzipped

Which bright spark insisted
That a dress should have its zip
Mostly located at the spine
Running from neck to hip?

Did they assume all women
And cross-dressers of this world
Would have a 24/7 partner
Or professional contortionist skills?

Or that we could simply sprout
A pair of extra-long arms
Like flaming Inspector Gadget
That extend beyond the norm?

You need to be an octopus
To zip yourself up alone
With a PhD in yoga
Like a coil cord from an old phone

The times I've almost slipped a disc
Trying to get my damn dress to fasten
Upside down, reaching for my butt
Bending over backwards

Twisting, turning, toiling
To no bloody avail
And still I can't yank the thing up
Much higher than my tail

Without really starting to wobble
Almost hitting the deck
Wrestling hard, cursing out loud
Profusely working up a sweat

It's really such a ball-ache
And to admit this I am loath
But frequently I leave the house
Indecently exposed!

Us

Some people are better off together
But we're better off apart
It doesn't mean I don't love you
But you're always breaking my heart

You refuse to let me in
Only briefly, but it never lasts
You close yourself to me
For you can't escape your past

I'm in awe of you as you know
But you're hurting and this you can't hide
So your numb yourself every day
To ignore what's really inside

You run away from yourself
For you hate who you really are
But this pain therein needs to heal
For your beauty lies in your scars

You need to love yourself
Or you'll sicken and eventually die
I've tried to make you better
But you're draining me all the time

You need to give something back
As I'm weakening every day
I can't sustain the two of us
If all you do is take

If I'm to stay
You need to change
And meet me at least halfway

Otherwise
We must say goodbye
For as things are I cannot stay.

Vicious Circle

The barbed cycle of abuse
Spins and turns
The perpetrator roams free
No lessons learnt

Constantly escaping
The scales of justice
Fiercely holding its victim
In its angry clutches

Caught in its web
Of control and manipulation
Bound by a billion threads
Powerless under its jurisdiction

Unable to think
Independently
The persecuted victim
Destroyed psychologically

No immunity to fight
The toxic onslaughts
Be they physical, emotional
Or their own Stockholm-syndrome like thoughts

Effectively caged and imprisoned
From systematic debasement
Lacking the self-belief
To fully escape the situation

The abuser in denial
Anything untoward took place
Adopting the 'victim' mentality
Now this spider has fallen from grace

Delusional to the hilt
The lies trip from its tongue
The threats pour forth in a torrent
Now its victim has tried to run

But the victim begins to falter
The road ahead unclear
Soiled and slippery from the oil slick
The abuser upon it did smear

Sliding backwards
Into the pit of despair
The victim weakens
Descending there

The arms outstretched
To save this poor mite
Not quite strong enough
To wrench the victim out of its plight

Thus the cycle
Engages once more
Spinning and turning
Just as before.

Virtual Vaginas

Sick of being objectified
By men just out for a f**k
Sick of vile predators
Baiting you and trying their luck

They project their fantasies on to you
Think you'll fulfil their needs
Ignoring the fact you have needs of your own
And you're not there just them to please

You're more than a mere vagina
A depository for them to release
You're a human being with feelings
Emotions and a history

You're worthy of love
You deserve respect
You're not a f***ing sex toy
To be disposed of when they're no longer erect

These people are vermin
So arrogant
Like ravenous beasts
On the hunt

For vulnerable prey
To entice into their trap
Where they trip you up
To get you flat on you on your back

Vultures that surf the net
And groom you via a dating sight
Try to lure you out, feigning affection
Crawling out of the shadows at night

It's all so twisted
Romance is dead
An elaborate ploy
To get you into bed

They may not quite be Weinstein
But it's in the same despicable vein
The abuse of women is rife
In this godforsaken digital age

Where are the gentlemen?
Where is their honour?
What happened to courting?
Getting to know one another?

Is this what it boils down to?
A flash in the pan?
Dehumanising females?
Wham bam, thank you, ma'am?

Shall we chop of our limbs?
Our torsos and heads?
For they're surplus to requirements
If we succumb to the likes of them!

Like Boxing Helena
If you break it right down
It makes my blood boil
That these diabolical clowns

Who should really hire a prostitute
Instead go all out online
In search of a bargain bang
Spinning their web of lies.

Wandering Hands In La-La Land

Wandering hands
Preying pervs
Surely now in La La Land
More will be unearthed

It's about time this rot
Was wheedled out
It shouldn't be what the profession
Is all about

The casting couch needs
To become obsolete
Shagging your way to the top
Never sat well with me

'Tis a plague on the profession
Afflicting women all too much
Why should we endure
Someone chancing a touch?

Groping you under the guise
It'll get you more work –
Don't these men realise
They are clearly sick jerks?

Abusing their power
And position in this way
Intimidating their victims
Into subjugation for pay

Thank God for Equity
If you have the balls to fight
I didn't once upon a time
But that doesn't make it right

Women must unite
And find their voice
Speak up and speak out –
You do have a choice!
#metoo

Waiting

Waiting for that call to come
Was like waiting for lockdown to end
As the minutes ticked by and I sat by the phone
I wondered if we were still friends

You only said might
And I took it for granted
It was a glimmer of light
And the seed was planted

But the call didn't come
And I cannot complain
You didn't make a promise
No need for you to explain

I'll just have to lower
My expectations
We're not on the same page
I'm not experiencing vexation

I was simply looking forward
After a long, lonely day
To having a conversation
And seeing your face

But you might be tired
Need time alone
I know that you're troubled
I'm not having a moan

I'll just have to distance
Myself a bit
I don't want to jump
Into a sinking ship

I offered you a lifeline
And that is all
That you didn't need to take it
Isn't your fault

It's tough being isolated
When the world is closed
All I ask, especially now,
Is that you don't raise my hopes.

Wasted Woman

Increasingly feeling invisible
Banging on doors that remain closed
Battling rejection
Frustrated and borderline morose

Emails and voicemails
That get no response
Wasted efforts
Over years, not just months

Money 'invested'
Seemingly poured down the drain
Hours spent labouring
Was it really all in vain?

What does one have to do?
To achieve that lucky break?
In the face of such fierce competition?
What the actual f**k does it take?

Is it my sex or my age?
Is it a sign of the times?
Will I ever get paid?
For formulating rhymes?

Will I ever get hired?
To tread again those wooden boards?
Will I ever again be admired?
By someone seeking more than a whore?

Should I have a mid-life crisis?
Delude myself I'm twenty once more?
Wear tiny skirts, platform stilettos
Pour myself into a size four?

It used to be easy
To magic up a job
To realise an ambition
Opportunities abounded in love

Anything was possible
Gambles nearly always paid off
Now I can't get a number on the lottery
Let alone five and the bonus ball!

I'm trying so hard
I really bloody am
But I keep hitting walls
Something is jammed

Being forty-odd and female
Is a tricky state to be in
Having neither wed nor bred
And no longer being young and thin

Is it time to chuck in the towel?
Wear tweed and a violet rinse?
For what I've got isn't what it takes
Thought admitting it makes me wince

Should all of us artistic women
Who just can't earn a crust
In the industry we love
Give up and gather dust?

Should we sulk in a corner?
With bitter, withering souls?
Because we never quite made it
And achieved our goals?

No we shouldn't
We should soldier on!
Do it the hell anyways
Because it's what we love!

We suffer for our art
And art imitates life
And life is tough at times
But at least we're living, right?

And the story isn't over
There are many chapters to be wrote
And while there's breath in your body
There's an element of hope

So don't give up,
Whether spinsters or sopranos!
We all are potential winners
One day we shall own Milanos!

Even if it's in our dreams
For without dreams we shrivel and die
So fight on to the death
Even if it means that we die trying!

What Box?!

If you try to box me in
I will come out fighting
Please don't try to mess with me
As I can be quite frightening

I'll take so much
And then I'll blow
Be warned of this
For there'll be nowhere to go

When I switch
To my fight mode
I'll take you down
As I explode

So you've been warned
For I've had enough
I may be blonde
But I can be tough

Don't be misled
By my bubbly disposition
I may appear fluffy
But you'll feel it if you're bitten

My teeth are sharp
And can cut to the bone
So you'd better back down
And leave me the f**k alone.

When The Dam Breaks

When the dam breaks
And your walls come down
And the tears flow in torrents
And there's no one around

Allow them to cascade
Down your cheeks
Don't stifle the flow
Don't think yourself weak

Know that you're cleansing
Releasing – just breathe
All those pent-up feelings
Simply decided to leave

Washing away the frustration
The hurts that you may have endured
Taking with them the toxins
As you surrender and purge

So cry it all out
And then cry some more
Don't withold one drop
Let that salt water pour

And when you're done
You'll feel so much lighter
Exhausted but at peace
You don't have to fight it

Then nurture yourself
Snuggle yourself up
And show yourself
Some affection and love.

When To Quit...

The actress that time forgot
Resting prolifically
Gathering rot

The craft that began to rust
As she waited in the shadows
Accumulating dust

The spotlight that eluded her so
After clinging tightly to her dreams
She had to let them go

The opportunities that didn't knock
But passed her by
With the ticking of the clock

The fire in her belly that wouldn't subside
Though nothing of note
Did materialise

The watching of others' success
As she pondered upon
Her own lack in distress

The waning of that ambition
Abandoned hope
Zero auditions

The conclusion it was time to quit
Try another avenue
Get over it

But this girl wasn't finished yet
She'd find her forte
Live without regret

For where there's a will there's a way
And when the sun rises
There's always another day.

Whose Rhyme Is It Anyway?

Dearest Friend
I love your bones
Not being lesbionic
I speak in platonic tones

You make me giggle
And warm my heart
You give me clothes
That you've fashioned with your art

A friend relatively new
But potent and valued a lot
A void you filled when the queen passed
A gesture that will never be forgot

I wish you'd have more confidence
And value yourself more
And see the gifts that you possess
And open up that door

To the beauty that lies within
And allow it to radiate out
See the diamond inside
And occasionally shut your mouth!

You generous person
You loyal soul
I hope you achieve your life's goal

You deserve the best
The universe has to reap
I wish you peace
And undisturbed sleep

Thank you for embracing me
And allowing me into your world
You're one very special lady
To this imperfect girl.

Wily Whippets

'Twas the dawn of Boxing Day
In misty Manningtree
The whole house was snoozing
When I awoke for a wee

So I had one of those
Then sought out my phone
But could I 'eck find it
Though all over did I roam

But in doing that
I accidentally
Left open the kitchen door
Setting Charlie free!

And the excited whippet
Couldn't believe his luck
As he shot towards the stairs
And like lightning bolted up

Galloping and gleeful
He sought out his humans
Who were soundly sleeping
Inside their rooms

With his generous snout
He nudged open their doors
As a mortified me
Stood there and watched

Oh Lord! thought I,
They'll be prematurely woke.
Somehow I must coax him
Downstairs – what a joke!

For he was dying to see them
As beloved were they to him
Thus he turned on his paws
And accelerated in

To the master bedroom
Disturbing Line
Who in being licked
Got a soggy surprise

She sleepily exclaimed
"What's the dog doing in here?"
As I quaked in my boots
Riddled with fear

I had to fess up
I was the culprit
Who'd left open the door
Releasing the whippet

Who now had to round him
Somehow back up
Re-deposit him in the kitchen
With its door firmly shut

But try catching a rogue whippet
Who's on the run
When you've had no caffeine
And you're not an Olympian

Farcical it was
Like *The Benny Hill Show*
As he ran a zillion rings around me
Because I was too flaming slow

Wearing me out
'Til I was in a sweaty heap
'Til I surrendered and went in search of a supersized coffee

Then the little tinker
Decided to follow me
To the target kitchen
Most obediently

So I seized the moment
Like carpe diem
Ferméd la port
Vowed never to open it again

Realised I was victorious
In a very roundabout way
Charlie was back in his boudoir
And the Djuve-Woods in bed could stay

The moral of this story
Is never try too hard
Everything will fall into place
Although whippets will you outsmart!

Winter In June

Winter in June
Thunderstorms and rain
Below-average temperatures
Wind that's insane

Plants topple over
Flowerpots smash
No need for sunscreen
More like scarves and hats

Umbrellas at the ready
Warm coats on
Dark, sulllen days
What's happened to the sun?!

Eating for comfort
Soups and stews
Too cold for salads
Need something hot inside of you

The ice cream shop
A barren place
No trips to the seaside
Instead we brace

Ourselves for the onslaught
Gather round the fire
Whack the heating back on
And feel unseasonably tired

Some snuggle up in bed
In front of the TV
No frolicking on patios
Or sunbathing

It's not usually this miserable
At this time of year
But what can we do?
Except play it by ear?

Wait for the dreariness
To subside
For the sun to resurface
Once the showers have dried

We simply must pray
The end will come soon
Of 2019's
Winter in June.

You Are Not Alone

On the edge of sanity
All screwed up inside
Mentally and physically
Wrung out and, oh, so tired

Anxiety overload
Questioning so, so much
Oversensitive
Frankly raw, in need of love,

Compassion and understanding
And time to sort this out
For I'm looking over the precipice
Hoping wings will somehow sprout

As I don't want to fall
I only wish to fly
I'm doing my very best
To soar into the sky

So don't be mad
If I seem distant
Give me a little space
And don't be too persistent

Or demanding of my time
I can't be 'there' for now
For I just need to unwind
Until I'm through this cloud

It's been building
For a while
Been struggling lately
To laugh and smile

Too much noise
Inside my head
Need to still
The cogs and rest

For I am human
And I have bipolar
They call it an
Affective disorder

I am not ashamed
To admit to this
The stigma needs to end
If it indeed exists

If you're suffering
Find your voice
Ask for help
This wasn't your choice

Invisible disabilities
Are so misunderstood
Often overlooked
Mishandled and, sadly, judged

But support is out there
If you can but ask
This I know
So speak up fast

Once you have
You'll feel so much better
And life will improve
You won't regret it

Enough now said
I've aired my piece
And frankly it was
A blessed release

Know I'm OK
But it's good to know who's there
I'm not far away
Just administering some self-care.

You Can Choose Your Friends...

A guilty plea
Judgement passed
Off virtually Scott free
The law is an ass!

Twelve-month conditional
Discharge – that's all!
And a lifetime of hell
Is what we've endured

In addition to that
Family politics explode
Brats with big mouths
Add to the load

No respect
For the victim's plight
Just one-upmanship
Jealousy and strife

With relatives like these
Blood ties are severed
Who needs enemies?
When you're kicked down in bad weather?

The lack of support
And empathy beggars belief
No wonder I live far away
What a blessed relief

I occasionally wonder
Why I left them all behind
Bar four there's nothing left
For me here to bind

So I'll return to The Smoke
When morning comes
Harbouring a refugee
Until she's rehomed

And get on with my life
'Cause Lord knows it's tough enough
To exist in a world
At times so devoid of love.

Zombie Zeitgeist

I confess I'm addicted to my phone
My observations tell me I'm not alone
For when you venture out it's plain to see
The majority of us are glued to our screens

Whether on the tube or pushing a pram
We all have devices in our hands
Surfing the net or social networking
Everyone obsessed with being plugged in

It's getting so bad even in company
We're not fully there as we view our screens
And now there are warnings from TFL
Not to fall down escalators as a result of this swell

In checking our messages, writing posts
Face-to-face interaction up in smoke
We'd rather be alone in the cyber world
Than engaging in reality with other boys and girls

It is an epidemic that's spreading extremely fast
Thus it seems that human contact could become a thing of the past
No need to leave the house anymore
When everything can be ordered and delivered to your door

A society of zombies isolated could we become
If we don't down devices and venture out into the scrum
And mingle with other beings physically there
Where we can look them in the eye and maintain that stare

Connecting on a basic level without the aid of Wi-Fi
And concentrating on each other instead of being distracted by
Notifications and little beeps
Incoming communication that never sleeps

And keeps you up all night as your brain just can't switch off
From all the incessant stimuli we're inundated with
Time to give it a rest, take a break just for a while
Look up from your laptops and perhaps give someone a smile

Watch where you are going, don't get yourself run over
Be present in the moment and you hopefully won't fall over
Have a coffee with someone instead of instant messaging
Regard the world around you taking note of everything

Don't zone out and go into a solitary trance
Assemble your tribe, spin some tunes, have a little dance
Limit your time on the world wide web
Grab yourself a hottie and get jiggy with them instead

I'm talking to myself
As well as anyone else
Your family and chums are precious
And deserve nothing less

Than your undivided attention
For one day there'll come a time
When perhaps they're no longer around
And you regret being online.

THE END

Rachel Rhodes-Puckett is a poet, actress, spiritualist
and self-proclaimed professional bimbette. This is her second
book, having self-published the first, entitled *The Pennings
Of The Poisonous Pixie's Book Of Poetry*, in 2017.

For more information on the author please visit
www.thepoisonouspixie.com.

Printed in Great Britain
by Amazon